THE WHOLE CHURCH

The Whole Church: Women, Leadership, The Church and Why it All Matters

www.thewaychurch.ca

Design by Arielle Ratzlaff

Library and Archives Canada Cataloguing in Publication

Title: The whole church : women, leadership, the church and why it all matters / Elita Friesen & Chris Price.
Names: Friesen, Elita, author. | Price, Chris (Preacher), author.
Identifiers: Canadiana 20210165200 | ISBN 9781990331008 (softcover)
Subjects: LCSH: Women in church work. | LCSH: Women in Christianity. | LCSH: Christian leadership.
Classification: LCC BV4415 .F75 2021 | DDC 253.082—dc23

THE WHOLE CHURCH

Women, Leadership, The Church and Why it All Matters

ELITA FRIESEN & CHRIS PRICE

For my Dad. I love you.
— Elita

For Michelle.
— Chris

FOREWORD

········· Darrell Johnson

At the time of writing this brief preface, I have been engaged in formal Christian ministry for over 50 years, both as pastor for various congregations (in the US, the Philippines and Canada) and as professor of pastoral theology and preaching (for both Regent College and Carey College in Vancouver). Over these years—decades—I have had the privilege of serving with many amazingly gifted women whom Jesus has called into discipleship and ministry. And I have spent much time with them as they work through their sense of call in light of their understanding of the authority of the Bible. For some, the wrestling has been deeply agonizing.

The arguments for and against women in various ministry positions demand care and patience with complexity. The emotions in the debates run deep, at times morphing into words and actions contrary to the whole of the Gospel in which we all, on both sides, seek to live our lives. At times one thinks, “Yes, that is exactly what God is saying in His word!” And, then at other times, “Maybe I am just imposing my own personal agenda, or the particular conviction of the culture at the present moment.”

My friends Elita Friesen and Chris Price have, from different angles, worked through the complexity, and have arrived at what they believe to be the way forward. An exciting way forward! As you will discover, both are sharp thinkers, faithful students of Scripture, eager for the whole church to be fully engaged in the whole of Jesus’ ministry in and for the world.

Elita and Chris unpack for us the trajectory set in the first page of the Bible that works its way through to the last page. Namely that both men and women are created in the image of God (Adam and Eve), that both men and women are called into the adventure of faith (hence, people like Abraham and Sarah), that both men and women have been set free by the Messiah and Lord (hence, people like Peter and Mary Magdalene) and that both men and women are empowered by the Holy Spirit to serve in all the ways the whole church is called to serve (hence, people like Pricilla and Aquila).

In his letter to disciples of Jesus living and working in the 1st century city of Ephesus, the apostle Paul speaks of five special gifts the Risen Christ gives to the whole church to enable the whole church to be alive in the Holy Spirit.

> And He [the ascended Jesus] gave some apostles, some prophets, some evangelists, some pastors and teachers.
>
> Ephesians 4:11

Why?

> For the equipping of the saints [disciples of Jesus being made holy] for the work of service, to the building up of the body of Christ.
>
> Ephesians 4:12

Now, here is the thing. All five of these gifts are exercised by both men and women in the Bible. As we read in the story of the emerging church in the book of Acts we see women serving as apostles. Women serving as prophets. Women serving as evangelists. Women serving as pastors. Women serving as teachers.

Because in Jesus Christ both women and men have been freed and gifted and called and empowered to serve with Him who is the Great Apostle, Prophet, Evangelist, Pastor and Teacher. He calls both women and men to participate in His on-going ministry in and for the world.

So, I invite you to now turn the page, and let my friends Elita and Chris lead you through the complexity of the issues into the vibrancy and joy of serving with the Great Servant.

INTRODUCTION

.... Elita & Chris

Our friend Melissa[1] is a gifted teaching pastor on staff at a church in Vancouver. One Sunday morning, after a particularly powerful message, several members of the church congregation made their way toward her to express their appreciation for the word she'd brought. Among those who paused to speak with her were a few older men who presented her with what they considered to be genuine encouragement. The first gentleman to reach her offered a smile and confidently said, "That was a pretty powerful sermon! Did your husband help you write it?" He was not making a joke or being sarcastic; he was genuinely wondering if her husband had in fact helped her to write the sermon. Attempting to hide her surprise, Melissa assured him that she had been able to put the message together without her

1 Name changed

husband's help. Amazingly, another gentleman offered very similar comments: "Well done! How much did your husband have to help you?"

When Melissa shared this unfortunate story with us, we felt compelled to ask an obvious question: would this have happened to a male teaching pastor? If Melissa's husband had preached the powerful message that day, would people have lined up to ask him if his wife had helped write the sermon? Our instincts tell us no. More than our instincts, I (Chris) have preached almost weekly for over ten years and, despite having all kinds of odd things said to me after speaking, no one has ever asked me if my wife helped me write my sermon. Strange double-standard, isn't it? One that, unfortunately, exists at many levels of society.

Gender Bias

In 2017 a study was published which indicated that, when it comes to the software coding community, women's contributions tend to be accepted more than men's when their gender is unknown.[2] When the gender is identifiable, however, the work of men was accepted at a higher rate. Though women have shown themselves to be incredibly competent coders, there seems to be a gender bias at work in the industry.

Many other studies have been cited to indicate a similar phenomenon. One famous example involves the orchestra. Orchestras were often male-dominated until they introduced blind

2 https://peerj.com/articles/cs-111/?utm_source=TrendMD&utm_campaign=PeerJ_TrendMD_0&utm_medium=TrendMD (Accessed Oct 24th, 2020)

auditions into the hiring process. Similar to the popular singing show *The Voice,* judges had to listen to the musician without any awareness of their appearance or gender. Some orchestras even introduced carpet on the stage to muffle the weight distribution of footsteps, apparently avoiding the possibility of determining gender by the creaking sound of the floorboards. The results of such efforts were illuminating. More and more women were accepted to play in orchestras, revealing a gender bias in the hiring process.

It is painful to consider the many ways in which women have been marginalized and mistreated historically. It is even more difficult to confront the reality that, despite great strides toward equality, it still continues today.

All is not doom and gloom, however. Though women continue to experience a "glass ceiling" in many fields of employment in our world, there has been significant progress in the western world. Our culture has slowly caught on to the fact that organizations tend to flourish when both men and women are in positions of significant influence, leading at the highest levels of the organization. There is also a growing body of data which shows that women are as effective, and in some areas more effective, than men at leading organizations. A survey of the leadership prowess of 2,780 senior leaders published in the Harvard Business Review in 2020 concluded that, "At every level, more women were rated by their peers, their bosses, their direct reports, and their other associates as better overall than their male counterparts—and the higher the level, the wider the gap grows... And two of the traits where women outscored men to the highest degree—taking initiative and driving for results—have long been thought of as particularly male strengths."[3] Other significant studies have produced similar results.[4]

The Church

As suggested by our opening story, for the Christian church it is also a mixed picture. Christianity has elevated the status of women throughout history and many of the first female rights advocates were women devoted to following Jesus. Many churches empower, equip and support women serving and leading in all areas of society. Countless women have found the church to be a place of healing, hope and help in times of difficulty. After all, 53 percent of the world's Christians are women and most available sources indicate that women do most of the mission and ministry globally. As Biblical scholar Graham Joseph Hill points out, "Women pray more than men, and are more likely to say that their faith and religion is important to them."[5]

At the same time the church hasn't always been hospitable towards the leadership gifts of women. For many Christians it is a source of great distress that the bias evidenced above can be felt in the church, especially in the area of female leadership and perhaps even more pointedly concerning women teaching and preaching. Christians have even been downright chauvinistic. One thinks of Anne Graham Lotz, Billy Graham's daughter,

---

3 Zenger and Folkman, "Are Women Better Leaders Than Men?"

4 In *Scaling Research*, Robert J. Anderson and William A. Adams explore decades of research into leadership effectiveness in both Fortune 500 companies and government agencies and they come to similar conclusions based on the data.

5 Graham Joseph Hill, *Holding Up Half the Sky: A Biblical Case for Women Leading and Teaching in the Church* (Eugene, OR: Wipf and Stock Publishers, 2020), xxi.

travelling to a pastor's conference to speak to men, only to have many of the participants turn their backs to her in the middle of her sermon in what appeared to be an organized protest to the public expounding of scripture by a woman. Less extreme, but still highly problematic, is the more recent example of Beth Moore being disrespected by a Christian leader on stage at a conference. It needs to be said that as long as prominent evangelicals can say publicly that excellent female Bible teachers like Beth Moore should "go home" and be greeted with ripples of laughter throughout the room, things need to change and repentance must take place in the evangelical church.

During earlier seasons of my (Chris's) life and ministry I would have condemned these examples as extreme, while believing this type of behaviour to be relatively rare. Conversation and experience have taught me differently. It is not just the more obvious hurdles or public slights. It is jumping on a conference call with other pastors and seeing only one or two women represented or, in many cases, no women present. It is walking into ministry settings knowing that as kind and cordial as others may be, a percentage of the room thinks women shouldn't be there and may even believe that their presence is a rebellion against God's natural order of things. It is the snide remarks or the well-meaning—perhaps innocently intended—comments that come off as condescending. It is the diminished opportunities. It is the loneliness of leadership compounded by all of the above.

I think of Naomi, a gifted woman called into church ministry. Although she was leading her first church by the age of 25, she encountered hurdle after hurdle that her other male colleagues never had to jump over. I remember sitting with her over coffee, listening to her story and marvelling at her giftedness and perseverance and long-suffering for the sake of Christ. Some time later, she sent me the following words she'd penned—words filled with the kind of pain, hope and raw honesty that gripped my heart:

She came here
In the same way he did
Their stories so interconnected
To Christ's Spirit and His Lordship
Yet
She was not welcome
A fact even her welcomers did not know
They were hospitable, they were authentic
There was nothing they did not do for a female
He was a leader though
History had taught them that
And maybe he was
Maybe not
But he appeared to be
Unlike she
In all her femininity
And emotional unpredictability...
But there were many who naively toed the line
"It doesn't really affect me, ya know, so it's fine..."
"Is it really a big deal for the Church's success?"
And little lonely she
On the tomato soaked soap box
Took a controlled breath
And said
"Yes"
"Yes, it is a big deal!

Yes, it does affect you!...
How many women do they need to see
Jesus send
In communion with men
To serve in ministry
To allow to kneel and learn at His Rabbi feet
To acknowledge as equal and not secondary?
How many?!
Too many
Says she.[6]

Our Church

Ten years ago I (Chris) wouldn't have been a natural person for Naomi to share with. Back then I believed in women in ministry, but I didn't think that women should lead at the highest levels of the church. I knew it was an unpopular position to hold in our culture, but I wore it like a badge of honour. Christians are not supposed to conform their thinking to society, I reasoned. We are to transform our minds through reading scripture and submitting to the word of God. And it seemed clear to me that scripture reserved certain areas of leadership in the church for qualified men only. I was convinced that I held this position while also loving and supporting many women in my life. After all, I was for women in vocational ministry; I was just not for women in all areas of ministry. I was for equality between the genders, but I wasn't for equity at all levels of church leadership—all because of my commitment to the authority of scripture.

6 Here is a link to Naomi's beautiful poem: https://www.thebeautyofdust.com/shesaid

After several more years of studying the Bible, reading different views, debating with friends and serving with remarkable, gifted women leaders far more skilled than me, I changed my mind. To be clear, I didn't change my mind about the authority of scripture, or the power and relevance of the Gospel, or about the wrath bearing, substitutionary death and bodily resurrection of Jesus, or about any of the essential doctrinal beliefs outlined in the major creeds of the early church. Rather, my perspective shifted in regard to what the Bible *actually* taught about women in ministry.

I decided I had been wrong. And, sadly, I had hurt people in the process.

So, when a team of us began to dream about planting a life-giving church in the heart of Vancouver, Canada it was important that, as a church, we would fully support the giftedness of women and we would welcome their full participation at all levels of leadership. This is because we believe the Bible both permits and encourages it, not because it happens to be more in-sync with the cultural mood regarding gender roles. It is our intention to have women leading at all levels of our church and to create a pipeline to train, encourage and empower men and women preachers, teachers, evangelists and leaders for the sake of the church in Canada and the advancement of God's mission in the world. And we do so in full awareness that some of our friends who lead thriving churches may not agree with us. As Darrell notes in the foreword, "The arguments for and against [women leading at all levels or ministry in the church] demand care and patience with complexity. The emotions in the debates run deep."

Although we can't answer every objection or cover every possible angle, and dear friends might still disagree with us once they finish these pages, this short book intends to provide a Biblical defense of our position as a church. In the pages to follow, we will engage in a brief survey of both the Old and New Testaments, highlighting the valuable contributions of women leaders, teachers and evangelists throughout the Biblical narrative. Then we will focus on the two most controversial scriptures that seem restrictive towards women preaching, teaching and leading in the church. Between chapters, Elita will not only share her own story, but spotlight significant women leaders in the Bible and throughout church history, moving the argument forward in a way that is fresh and applicable for the reader.

We believe the conclusion argued for in this short book are beneficial for numerous reasons: (1) It is the best understanding of the entire New Testament witness, which is crucial because culture does not establish our criteria for truth—Christ and His Word do. (2) It helps us avoid inflicting unnecessary wounds on women in the church who feel called to teach and lead—wounds that are both numerous and festering in the body of Christ. (3) It empowers women and affirms the fullness of their giftedness for the benefit of the whole church—and as the western world gets increasingly more secular we really do need *all* hands on deck. Without fully releasing women in the global church we are attempting to serve and change the world with one arm tied behind our back. (4) It is helpful for the church's witness in the western world. To put it bluntly, though it is important, the matter of women in church leadership is not a salvation issue. No individual's eternal destiny rests on their position regarding women in certain positions of church leadership; rather, redemption depends on God's saving grace, expressed in the atoning death and finished work of Christ on the cross, which is personally experienced by us through repentance and faith. Therefore, as missionaries to a western culture that finds it deeply repugnant to believe or even conceive of women being limited in the use of their teaching, preaching and leadership gifts (given how obviously competent they are at all of the above!), it would seem wise to adopt a perspective that errs on the side of freedom, especially when it results from a compelling reading of the entire New Testament witness. This type of missiological consideration doesn't drive the exegesis of this short book, but it is one significant and noteworthy benefit that flows from the argument unpacked in the pages that follow.

In the end, the perspective argued for in this book takes into account the work of the Holy Spirit through capable women preachers, missionaries, church planters and leaders in the global church. It honours the many, many women who have been called by God to preach and teach in their local congregations in a way that allows all to directly benefit.

And that is no small thing.

SPOTLIGHT:

ELITA'S STORY

······ Elita ······

I'll never forget the day I was invited to join the teaching team for The Way Church. My husband and I sat across from one of their pastors and listened as he began to validate things in me I'd privately, and painstakingly, surrendered to the Lord over the years. Not only did he take time to point out my God-given gifts and encourage my calling, he went on to emphasize that it was because I was a woman—not despite it—that what God had put in me was needed at this hour within the church. "Simply put, we believe in God's calling on your life," he said. Somehow, I managed to keep in the tears and utter a simple, but very genuine, "Thank you."

It's important to know that I never went looking to become a leader within the church. I certainly never felt any kind of draw to "prove" that women can do everything in the church that men can do. Actually, I grew up in a beautiful church environment consisting primarily of Godly, humble men in leadership who honoured and esteemed women. It was probably because I was exposed to this model that it just never dawned on me that a woman could, or should, be behind a pulpit teaching or preaching. In fact, my dad was the senior pastor of our church and he was the one to put me on the Sunday morning platform as a young worship leader. He was the one who introduced me to music and books by strong Christian female leads. He never told me I couldn't because I was a girl. He never told me to aim "a little lower" than my big brother. All my dad told me in regard to my calling was to steward well the gifts God had put in me and trust the Lord with the rest.

I never had an "ah-ha" moment, as many people seem to have, where I sensed an overwhelming call into ministry. Instead, when I was in my mid-twenties I had what I would call a "perhaps" moment. I remember that I was sitting on my bedroom floor while my young boys napped, Bibles and commentaries spread out on the carpet all around me in preparation for a women's Bible study I was leading, and I had this very clear thought: I want to spend my life doing this. Perhaps, Lord, you could use me.

When it became clear that my passion was for studying and teaching scripture, I had to wrestle through some tough questions about what I believed; I wondered why God would give me a gift that was useless within the church or, at least, was better suited for a man. At no point did it occur to me that I would ever talk on a stage or, gulp, behind a pulpit on a Sunday. Those thoughts were far too lofty and, honestly, I don't think I knew how I really felt about women being in a primary leadership role within the church. But here's what I did come to terms with that day as I sat on my floor, doubt flooding my soul like a tidal wave: perhaps God had called me to teach. I didn't know in what capacity. I didn't start imagining scenarios. I just decided to quietly submit to His teaching and His timing. I committed to working hard, taking classes, sitting under sound theological doctrine and learning as much as I could, and I aimed to go to seminary.

Fast-forward a decade and no one is more shocked than I am at the places where God has positioned me. Through no doing of my own, no forcing my way in, the Lord has graciously opened doors to me. And though I do not see myself as any kind of trailblazer, I am a Christ-follower, wholly committed to going where He leads me. I can't speak for all women, but I can clearly say of myself: it has never been and will never be my intent to replace a man's role within the church. It is, however, my whole-hearted desire to use the gifts God has entrusted to me (2 Timothy 1:14) for the good of His Kingdom in our generation. Through my own experience, through the study of scripture and by sitting under the teaching of theologically sound pastors and professors, I have concluded that God not only created me with gifts and a calling, but that He fully endorses the proper use of them in His church.

To those in the next generation of women who have sensed a call on their life but have felt conflicted or confused over the role of women in the church, I pray this book breathes fresh life into you. May you feel encouraged to lean into the gifts God has put inside of you, seeking to steward them well. Being a woman in no way excuses us from treating the call to teach or pastor as anything less than holy; all who feel a call to teach should be committed to learning and growing and sitting under sound theological teaching. And though the idea of women in leadership may remain a tough subject within the church, and though it may feel like an uphill battle at times, may you and I both remember that God did not make a mistake when He put the gift of leadership inside of us. But let us also remember that we have an opportunity before us to be a generation of women who don't rise because men fall. Rather, let us set a new standard that seeks to honour men. It is not us against them. It is us *with them* for the sake of the Gospel. Who knows? Perhaps—like Esther—we were created for such a moment as this.

CHAPTER 1
WOMEN IN THE OLD TESTAMENT

········· Elita & Chris

The best place to start is usually the beginning. And not just at the beginning of our story, but at the beginning of all stories.

Most cultures have their own unique story of beginnings that speaks to human dignity and destiny or lack thereof.

In one African creation story a giant gets sick and vomits out creation: the sun, the moon, the stars, vegetation and, finally, human beings.

In the Babylonian creation myth called "The Enuma Elish" the world is created from the dismembered limbs of a god and the world is then birthed in divine violence—humanity is made only as an after-thought to serve the gods.

One dominant narrative for many people today, particularly

in the secular Western world, involves a universe catapulted into existence from nothing. From this phenomenon, unconscious matter produces consciousness, order evolves from disorder, and non-life gives birth to life. There is no objective meaning to the cosmos, and love is an accidental by-product of a meaningless collision of atoms, a brief twinkling of light in an otherwise dark, cold, relatively empty universe.

But when we turn to the creation story found in the Bible we discover a drastically different narrative. Here we learn of one God who speaks the cosmos into existence through the power of His Word. The earth is formless and void and His Spirit hovers over the chaos, intentionally bringing order out of the disorder. We read of God's great delight in His handiwork as the story repeatedly tells us that "God saw that it was good." This rhythmic refrain, repeated no less than five times, reads like an artist rejoicing over a masterpiece. And though everything He had made had indeed been good, the story reaches a climactic point with the creation of humanity, which God declares to be *very* good! Genesis 1:26-27 tells us:

> Then God said, "Let us make humankind in our image, in our likeness, so that they may rule over the fish in the sea and the birds in the sky, over the livestock and all the wild animals, and over all the creatures that move along the ground." So God created mankind in his own image, in the image of God he created them; male and female he created them.

Men and women are created in the "image and likeness of God"—created "very good" by their Maker. It is a beautiful story, a breath of fresh air when compared to other ancient Near Eastern cosmogonies, but what relevance does it have to the issue of qualified women serving at all levels of church leadership?

The rest of this chapter will be devoted to answering that question.

The Image of God

According to Genesis 1, nothing else in creation is made in the image of God. The image of God sets humanity apart from the rest of the animals. The fact that *everyone* is made in the image of God separates *this* story from other creation stories in the ancient world where only the king is made in the image of God. This represents a radical democratization of God's image applied to all of humanity, male and female, ruler and ruled. Throughout church history many have sought to equate the image of God with our reason, or our morality, or anything that seems to separate us from the animal world. Most of this work, though helpful and true in many respects, was rooted in Greek philosophy and not in the Biblical text as it stands. To truly comprehend what it means to be made in the image of God it is important to understand the ancient Near East, which is the world in which the Biblical creation story first appeared. Dr. Iain Provan, scholar of Old Testament studies, writes:

> Human beings are to 'rule' the created order. In the ancient Near East, such rule was exercised by the gods through their temple images. Their authority was further delegated to the king who was considered to be 'like a god.' The king was the god's right-hand man. Genesis, in contrast, says it is the destiny of human beings to rule over the cosmos. It is, moreover, the

> destiny of human beings all together to rule. Since every human is made in God's image, each embodies God's presence in his temple-cosmos and represents him there.[1]

The creation account in Genesis, therefore, tells us that we are all royalty. Psalm 8 echoes this truth when the psalmist rightly pushes against the ancient Near Eastern stories and says of the Lord, "What is mankind that you are mindful of them, human beings that you care for them? You have made them a little lower than the angels and crowned them with glory and honour. You made them rulers over the works of your hands; you put everything under their feet." We are, then, a humanity made in God's image, called to reflect God's character, and we are to rule God's world as His royal representatives creating a culture that honours Him and promotes human flourishing in a loving relationship with the Creator.

The story continues in Genesis 2 where Adam and Eve are put into the garden to "work it and keep it" (Gen. 2:15). Dr. Provan emphasizes these terms as "priestly language".[2] Human beings, as God's royal representatives, are entrusted with a holy responsibility: taking care of God's good world.

Further to the point, these two words "work" and "keep" appear thirteen other times in the Old Testament and all but two of the occurrences refer to some type of worship. Greg Beale, an expert on temple theology in scripture, points out that the garden-sanctuary acts as a prototype for the tabernacle, which in turn foreshadows the temple. The book of Numbers uses the

---

1 Iain Provan, *Seriously Dangerous Religion* (Waco, TX: Baylor University Press, 2014), 83-84.
2 Ibid., 224.

same language found in Genesis when it says of the tabernacle priests, "And they shall *keep* his charge, and the charge of the whole congregation before the tabernacle of the congregation, to *do the service* of the tabernacle" (Numbers 3:7 KJV, emphasis added). Therefore, Adam and Eve were not only called to rule over creation as kings and queens submitted to the ultimate rule of God, they were also commissioned to engage in a *priestly* ministry. At the beginning of the Biblical narrative this dignity was placed on the shoulders of men and women: equal in worth, equal in dignity, equal in function and equal in destiny. From Genesis 1 and 2 we learn that the intended divine order was that men and women would be under God, over creation and side-by-side creating God-honouring culture together as equals. The original picture is not about men ruling women or women ruling men, or men replacing women or women replacing men. It is men and women ruling and serving together as royalty in God's world. More than that, men and women are royal priests in God's temple of creation.

A Helper Suitable?

In Genesis 2 we also see that the woman is made from the side of the man:

> But for Adam no suitable helper was found. So the Lord God caused the man to fall into a deep sleep, and while he was sleeping, he took one of the man's ribs and closed up the place with flesh. Then the Lord God made a woman from the rib he had taken out of the man, and he brought her to the man.
>
> Genesis 2:20-22

She is made to be man's helper, but this description entails no belittlement or subservience. In fact, ezer, the Hebrew word translated as "helper", is most frequently used to describe God in the Old Testament. Scholar Alvera Mickleson notes that in the Bible the word ezer is never used of a subordinate.[3] Of the 20 times this word is used in the Old Testament, 17 times it is used to refer to God as our helper—not meaning that God is our subordinate, but that God is our strength or power. Here we see the woman taken from the side of the man and that is where she belongs. Not behind him in denigration. Not in front of him in domination. But side-by-side as equals, loving, serving and worshiping God together.

The Fall

Sadly, in Genesis 3 sin enters the world and everything changes. The beautiful picture of equality painted in Genesis 1 and 2 is threatened and a society where men (more often than not) ruled women was set into motion. In Genesis 3 this new reality is described when God says to the woman, "Your desire will be for your husband, and he will rule over you" (Genesis 3:16). A husband ruling over his wife is the result of the fall into sin and does not reflect God's original ideal for the relationship between husband and wife and men and women.

Throughout the rest of the Old Testament narrative we undeniably encounter the patriarchal bent of the ancient Near East where men dominated the political, religious and familial

---

3 Stanley J. Grenz & Denise Muir Kjesbo, *Women in the Church: A Biblical Theology of Women in Ministry* (Downers Grove, lll: Intervarsity Press, 1995), 164.

landscape. As we do, we must keep in mind that scripture is often descriptive (this is what happened) not prescriptive (this is what *should* have happened): scripture is true to history and shows how God interacts with His people within their fallen culture. God meets people where they are, even making concessions to hardened hearts to lead them to where He wants them to be. A great example of this is Jesus' take on Moses' laws about divorce in Matthew 19:4-10. Jesus teaches that these laws were a provisional concession to the hardness of people's hearts, and then references the creation story to establish God's ideal for the husband/wife relationship. God's intention is always to draw His people back toward His original ideal of human flourishing as described in Genesis 1 and 2, and this includes the relationship between men and women. And despite the male-dominated bent of ancient societies, within Israel there are still multiple examples of women leading and exercising spiritual authority alongside men, as was God's intention in the very beginning. Below we'll highlight a few brief examples.

Female Leaders

During the time period of the Judges, God raised Deborah up as an exceptional judge and leader of Israel.[4] Her leadership skills and influence were unquestionable. As Scott McKnight quips, Deborah was "the president, the pope, and Rambo all bundled up in one female body."[5] After leading Israel to victory in battle she acted as a judge over Israel in the hill country near Bethel, a

4 Judges 4,5
5 Scott McKnight, *The Blue Parakeet: Rethinking How You Read the Bible* (Grand Rapids, MI: Zondervan, 2008), 168.

location that is both meaningful and strategic throughout scripture (Judges 4:5). Significantly, the description of her ministry in Judges 4:5 is very reminiscent of the language used to describe the ministry of Moses. The narrator in Judges writes that, "all the Israelites came up to her for judgment." To quote Denise Kjesbo, "As the mediator of public disputes, she, like Moses before her, served a public role in a public realm."[6] There are other moments in Israel's history where women exercise significant political authority and leadership like Deborah. Another example would be Athaliah who ruled the land of Israel from 842 BC to 836 BC (2 Kings 11:3). And, in the intertestamental period, Salome Alexenderia was an honoured queen of the Hasmonean dynasty, ruling Judea from 76 to 67 BC.[7]

Female Prophets

The role of a prophet was very distinct in the Old Testament. A prophet proclaimed the word of God as a spiritual leader of God's people. A prophet had profound spiritual authority and there were several female prophets who played a significant role amongst God's people. Huldah was a prophetess who instructed both men and women.[8] Huldah prophesied during the same time as Jeremiah and had a prominent role in the political and religious life of God's people. "Huldah provided... leadership during the time of the divided monarchy. Although there were other prestigious prophets around (e.g., Jeremiah, Zephaniah,

---

6 Grenz, Kjesbo, *Women in the Church: a Biblical Theology of Women in Ministry* (Downers Grove, lll: Intervarsity Press, 1995), 69.

7 Editor, James R. Beck, *Two Views on Women in Ministry* (Grand Rapids, MI: Zondervan Academic, 2005), 52.

8 2 Kings 22:14

Nahum, and Habakkuk), it was Huldah's counsel concerning the Book of the Law that King Josiah sought out (2 Kings 22:11-14)."[9] More than that, it was Huldah's wise counsel that inspired and led to religious reforms in the community of Israel—reforms that reestablished the value of true prophets in the religious life of Israel (2 Chronicles 34:14-33).

A Male Priesthood

Everyone would likely grant the above examples of female leaders. Nevertheless, some would point out that the Old Testament priesthood was open only to qualified males and on this basis would suggest that, though they did serve in various areas of ministry, women shouldn't be in the highest positions of spiritual leadership or exercise authority in the religious community.

We don't find this to be a compelling argument.

The Old Covenant priesthood was tethered inextricably to the tabernacle and temple system, both of which have been fulfilled in Christ and are no longer necessary. This makes it doubtful that the pattern of an all-male priesthood should have any continued theological bearing on the New Testament church and therefore on women's place in leadership. This conclusion is reinforced by the fact that one of the reasons women were forbidden to engage in priestly ministry was due to the nature of the Old Covenant purity laws regarding the discharge of blood, which rendered women "unclean" on a cyclical basis. While these regulations remain confusing and off-putting for us as modern people, certain bodily discharges for both men and

---

9 Editor, James R. Beck, *Two Views on Women in Ministry* (Grand Rapids, MI: Zondervan Academic, 2005), 52.

women rendered them religiously unclean under the Levitical laws. Again, these laws have been fulfilled by and abolished in Christ and do not carry forward into the New Covenant era in which we live, thereby removing another of the reasons women were excluded from the Old Covenant priesthood. In addition, the original mandate of humanity, applied to men and women alike, *was* to be priestly rulers over all of creation; in the New Testament the entire church is referred to as a kingdom of *priests*. Peter writes of the New Testament church, "You are a chosen people, a royal priesthood, a holy nation, a people belonging to God, that you may declare the praises of him who called you out of darkness into his wonderful light" (1 Peter 2:9). Women are certainly part of this royal priesthood. This fact, and the evidence already described in which the leading, teaching and prophetic giftedness of various women was not forbidden in the Old Testament, makes it highly suspect to build a case *against* women in leadership from the limited, time-bound fact of an all-male priesthood under the Old Covenant.

Conclusion

In the very beginning God gave women the same priestly calling as men and, even in our fallen world, we witness them exercising authority—both politically and spirituality—as God intended from the start. And we have seen in this brief survey that women clearly functioned in significant leadership roles throughout the Old Testament. These occasions, though not near as frequent as modern people would like, never come with any hint of God's disapproval. If they are exceptions, they are exceptions that appear to be blessed and empowered by God—all of which we would expect if God was calling women to lead in what was an overwhelmingly male-dominated culture. This continues on a heightened scale when we arrive at the New Testament. With the coming of Jesus we enter into a time of increasing freedom for men and women to operate in ministry through the outpouring of the Holy Spirit.

SPOTLIGHT:

THE LIFE OF MIRIAM

...... Elita ......

As we have just seen, the Old Testament includes capable women God used in obvious leadership positions. One woman whom we have not yet mentioned, but who is extremely significant in the Old Testament narrative, is Miriam. While she is undoubtedly most well-known as the older sister of Moses, Miriam's life is documented in the Old Testament through three pivotal moments: as a courageous young girl who helped save her baby brother, as a joyful adult who co-led the Israelites in the song of victory after crossing the Jordan River, and finally, quite anticlimactically, as a jealous older sister. Miriam's life has some sober lessons to teach us, not only on the issue of women in church leadership, but also concerning leadership in general.

In Exodus chapter 2 we find Miriam as a young girl who courageously risked her life as she kept watch over her illegally-hidden baby brother, Moses. At her mother's urging, Miriam defied Pharaoh's kill-order and protectively "stood at a distance to see what would happen to (Moses)" (2:4). She then boldly approached the daughter of the one who wanted her brother dead and initiated a brilliant plan that ultimately allowed her brother to be fostered by his very own birth family. Although we are not told in scripture how she arrived at this plan, what can undoubtedly be agreed upon is this: Miriam had to choose bravery when the moment presented itself. This would have been no small task, especially for an adolescent Hebrew girl in the presence of Egyptian royalty. It might have been tempting to remain at a safe distance and simply watch what happened to her brother. It might have been tempting to walk away after it became clear Pharaoh's daughter was taking pity on Moses and he'd survive. Miriam could have turned toward home knowing her brother's life had been spared, but she kept moving forward. As God was moving the necessary pieces into position for the coming deliverance of His people, Miriam's role was crucial. God chose to work in and through the obedience of this young girl.

Of course, Miriam had no idea at the time who Moses would grow up to be; she had no knowledge of the call on her brother's life or that he was the one God would use to deliver Israel. It was the very lack of this knowledge that made her selfless sacrifice all the sweeter. Having a role in helping to both save and steer his life must have been a badge of honour she wore for the rest of her life. Even as a young girl Miriam proved to be clever, unselfish and courageous—all the makings of a leader.

Miriam is not mentioned again until Exodus 15, after the Israelites have crossed the Red Sea and escaped from Egypt. Miriam's role is a bit more magnified as she, along with her now-grown brother Moses, lead the people in a song to the Lord immediately after their deliverance. Not only is this the first song recorded in the Bible, but what increases its significance is the fact that the song occurred as an organic response—it wasn't a mustered-up song or a set of lyrics that took days or months to write. The song was led by Moses and Miriam out of the pure overflow of their hearts in a divine moment. It is likely that Moses led the Israelites in the first part of the song and Miriam led the women in the second part. It would have been an honour for anyone—but especially a woman—to be promoted into such a public role in the Israelite community.

Miriam's role is further magnified in Exodus 15 when she is referred to as a prophet, similar to her other brother, Aaron. In the Old Testament, "Hebrew prophets primarily anticipated the punishment of evil and/or a better life on earth for faithful Israelites. They spoke the truth about the present and what would happen if people did not change their behaviour and return to Yahweh's ways."[1] In other words, Miriam's place among the people as a prophet was not a light-weight position. Yet we do not read of any of the Israelites protesting; no one suggested it was inappropriate for a woman to take on this position. God Himself appointed her as a leader among the Israelites, not disqualifying her because of her gender. In Micah 6:4 the Lord says to Israel, "I brought you up out of Egypt and redeemed you from the land of slavery. I sent Moses to lead you, also Aaron and Miriam."[2]

Unfortunately, Miriam's story goes a bit sideways at this point. Toward the end of her otherwise humble life, we see jealousy emerge in her heart. It is no accident that every instance of Miriam being mentioned in the Bible coincides with the life of her brother, Moses. Perhaps she felt out-ranked or left in the shadows. No matter what led to her jealousy, Numbers 12 recounts her and her brother Aaron's final opposition to Moses: "'Has the Lord spoken only through Moses?' they asked. 'Hasn't he also spoken through us?'" (v. 2). What may have seemed like a simple complaint actually reeked of pride. The Lord took Miriam and Aaron to task over their self-righteousness and the Lord's "anger burned against them" (v.9).

As a further consequence, Miriam was struck with leprosy; it

---

1 Paul Redditt, "Prophets, the," ed. John D. Barry et al., *The Lexham Bible Dictionary* (Bellingham, WA: Lexham Press, 2016).
2 Emphasis added

was only at Moses' request that the Lord allowed her leprosy to be lifted after seven days. This is the last time Miriam is mentioned until her death in Numbers 20.

All leaders, male and female alike, can learn a sober lesson about pride from the life of Miriam: although jealousy, self-regard and ego run rampant in our flesh, for those of us within the church—especially in church leadership—our task is to weed it out before it chokes us out. Miriam failed to kill the pride that crept in and, sadly, her otherwise beautiful story ends on a note of decline.

I also want to humbly suggest that the way Miriam's life unfolded offers us a specific lesson for women in church ministry. To my female friends involved in or looking to become involved in ministry, I pray Miriam's story reminds us all of the cost of jealousy. While jealousy can rear its ugly head in different ways, many of us do what Miriam did: we start to grumble. We start to question. We start to think, "Why him or her or them and not me?" To be clear, I don't necessarily think Miriam was jealous because Moses was a man. I think it's plausible she could have been jealous for other reasons—perhaps of his title, his position among the people, or maybe even of his relationship with the Lord. "WHY NOT ME, TOO?" is the question she was ultimately asking. And it's the same question many females in the church are asking today. I want to take a moment to gently caution us all: very rarely does God respond to our "this isn't fair" mantra; much more often He responds to our "I'll serve right where I am, as unto the Lord" attitude. My prayer for our generation is that we would serve alongside the men and women God has assigned to us, esteeming them as co-labourers, not competition. If we are willing to accept Miriam's life as proof that God isn't gender-biased, then we must also be willing to accept that He gifts and He disciplines equally. May we be women who learn to embrace humility and uproot any trace of pride in our lives.

I appreciate the imperfect nature of Miriam's story. Unlike many of the women highlighted in scripture, Miriam's life flowed somewhat backward: she displayed courage and bravery at the start of her life—willing to risk her own life for that of her brother, she stepped into a role as a leader and prophet in the Israelite community—a beautiful example of God's inclusion of women, but her story is then sadly concluded as God deals with her pride. It was, however, ultimately through her failures that the redemptive nature of God was magnified. Although her pride and imperfection could have permanently disconnected her from the family of God, we witness her mercifully welcomed back into covenant community (Numbers 12:15). We see equal parts humanity in Miriam and grace in God; He graciously uses a young, willing girl. He graciously anoints and appoints that same grown woman to lead and prophecy over His chosen people. Then He graciously deals with her pride, disciplining her, but compassionately welcoming her back into the family.

It must be said that Miriam's life cannot and should not be reduced to a simple lesson on women in ministry. Ultimately, her life points to a much bigger gospel picture of a redemptive, good God who positions people for the good of His plan in every generation.

CHAPTER 2
WOMEN IN THE NEW TESTAMENT

········· Elita & Chris

The pop star Katy Perry has a tattoo of the name "Jesus" on her wrist. She once said, "I got this Jesus tattoo on my wrist when I was 18 because I know that it is always going to be a part of me. When I'm playing, it is staring right back at me saying, 'Remember where you came from.'"

Whether it is Katy Perry, Chance the Rapper, Justin Bieber, Kanye West or the lyrics from Coldplay's latest album, the person of Jesus continues to exert a magnetic pull on the hearts and imaginations of cultural icons and influencers. Though there is a distressing tendency to refashion Jesus in our own image and likeness, one of the reasons why Jesus remains popular is His care and compassion for people, especially those on the outside of mainstream society, which in His day certainly included women. In what follows we will investigate how Jesus elevated the status of women in the 1st century.

Jesus

Jesus' approach to women in ministry was revolutionary in His day. In the Jewish culture of the time it wasn't uncommon for rabbis to say horrible things about women. For example, a prominent rabbi once stated that, "The words of Torah should be burned rather than taught to a woman."[1] Jewish men were taught a daily prayer of thanksgiving for the fact that they weren't born as a woman. The highly authoritative Jewish writings known as the Talmud also say, "Sooner let the words of the Law be burnt than delivered to a woman," and, again, "Happy is he whose children are males, and woe to him whose children are females." The Jewish Historian Josephus, writing in the 1st century, states, "But let not the testimony of women be admitted...nor let servants be admitted to give testimony."

Pause for a moment and let the tragic nature of these comments sink in. For people living in the 21st century who have mothers and sisters and daughters, the degree of belittlement and disdain is hard to bear. For women who feel called to preach and teach in religious communities it is not just a painful reminder of degrading attitudes toward women—it may be salt in an open wound. Nevertheless, this type of attitude was common in the 1st century.

In light of this cultural context, Jesus' treatment of women was remarkable. While the mission of His life was not about

---

1 *Yerushalmi, Sotah* 3:4. A version of this story also appears in the Bavli, Yoma 66b

promoting some sort of modern feminist movement, Jesus did continuously give dignity, respect and honour to women. Let us start by considering the first woman Jesus would ever encounter: His mother. According to the familiar passage found in Luke 1, God sent the angel Gabriel to Mary with this declaration: "You have found favour with God. You will conceive and give birth to a son, and you are to call him Jesus. He will be great and will be called the Son of the Most High" (Luke 1:30-32a). This was the news the Jewish people, indeed the world, had been waiting for. And it was Mary, a young adolescent girl, who was the *first* person to be told the news of the coming Messiah. God invited a woman into the greatest story that would ever be told, strategically put her right near its center, and entrusted His only son to her.

By the time He began His public ministry, Jesus was known for allowing women to sit at His feet as disciples, something that no Jewish rabbi of that day would have done. One well-known example involves the story of Mary and Martha. In Luke 10, we see Mary sitting at Jesus' feet learning from Him in the posture of a disciple: "As Jesus and his disciples were on their way, he came to a village where a woman named Martha opened her home to him. She had a sister called Mary, who sat at the Lord's feet listening to what he said."[2] To quote respected New Testament scholar, Stanley Grenz:

> In contrast to many rabbis who considered it inappropriate to instruct women, Jesus readily taught them. Perhaps the most obvious example is Mary of Bethany, who sat at Jesus' feet (Lk. 10:39). In describing the scene, the Evangelist chooses terminology associated with rabbinic study (compare Acts 22:3),

2 Luke 10:38-39

> suggesting that Mary became Jesus' student....he defied the practice of excluding women from the study of Torah.[3]

Keep in mind that it was assumed in Jewish culture that, if you were invited to be a disciple of a rabbi, it was expected that you would also become an eventual teacher of Torah yourself. A rabbi had a "yoke", a set of teachings, that would be passed on to his disciples who would, in turn, pass it on to others. As Graham Joseph Hill points out, "One sits at the feet of a teacher in order to become a teacher. Talk about a dramatic challenge to the prevailing limitations on women, and to the norms of culture!"[4] Though Mary wasn't one of the twelve disciples, she clearly sat in the position of a disciple to her Rabbi, Jesus. When Mary's own sister challenged the legitimacy of her place at Jesus' feet, Jesus gave this gentle rebuke: "Mary has chosen what is better, and it will not be taken away from her."[5] In a first-century Jewish society where the study of Torah was reserved only for boys and men, it was a powerful act for Jesus to state firmly that 'it will not be taken away from her'.[6]

Jesus also empowered women to represent Him as evangelists. His first missionary to the Samaritans was the woman at the well in John 4 who had a difficult past. Think of the quotes we read earlier:

---

3 Stanley J. Grenz & Denise Muir Kjesbo, *Women in the Church: A Biblical Theology of Women in Ministry* (Downers Grove, ILL: Intervarsity Press, 1995), 75.

4 Graham Joseph Hill, *Holding Up Half the Sky: A Biblical Case for Women Leading and Teaching in the Church* (Eugene, OR: Wipf and Stock Publishers, 2020), 21.

5 Luke 10:42b

6 Kate Cooper, *Band of Angels: The Forgotten World of Early Christian Women* (New York, NY: Overlook Press, 2013), 42.

"Don't teach women the law!"

"Don't let women testify!"

"Don't talk to women in public!"

Jesus ignores it all. He essentially says to this woman, "Here is the most precious news in human history, and I want you to hear it first: I am the Messiah! I am the Saviour! I am the Promised One!" Amazingly, she learned His true identity before it had been revealed to His disciples. In fact, Jesus' disciples were surprised to find Him talking to a woman in public at all, regardless of the topic. This woman went on to be the first person to proclaim the good news of Jesus to the men and women in her hometown, sparking a revival where "many came to believe" (John 4:39-42).

Another striking example of Jesus' inclusion of women comes from the resurrection narratives found in the Gospels. On the Sunday after Jesus' crucifixion when He rose from the dead, he appeared to His 12 disciples (minus Judas). But even before that Jesus appeared to two women! These women were the original proclaimers of the resurrection and they preached this good news to the disciples making them, in the words of Thomas Aquinas, "apostles to the apostles"! Jesus initially entrusted the most important news in all of human history to women, and He did this in a Jewish culture that did not trust the testimony of women. The resurrected Lord, as His first act, thumbed His nose at the chauvinism entrenched in 1st century Judaism and rebuked the disciples for "their stubborn refusal to believe those who had seen him after he had risen."[7]

---

7 Mark 16:14

But The Twelve Disciples Were All Men

Despite the prominence of women in Jesus' ministry it is true that He chose twelve male disciples to be leaders in His movement. Some might make the case that Jesus' selection of the twelve means that it is inappropriate for women to lead at the highest level in the church, but we want to suggest this may be missing the point. It is more likely that, in choosing twelve male disciples, Jesus was both symbolically and actually reconstituting a 'new Israel' around His person (not a replacement of Israel, but a fulfilment of their story, centered around Jesus, that would now include Gentiles as well), and it makes sense that He would pick twelve men to represent the twelve sons of Jacob, the originators of the twelve tribes. One could also make the case that Jesus' selection of twelve male disciples was a culturally expedient way of getting His message out to the masses, given the lack of respect afforded to women in the Jewish culture of the day. In addition, keep in mind that Jesus travelled and lived in close quarters with His twelve disciples and the fact that they were all men would have avoided unnecessary scandal.

Jesus often flouted cultural conventions for the sake of His message, as He did in the case of the woman at the well or in the example of the empty tomb mentioned above, and those moments when he did so hold tremendous significance. Other times Jesus worked redemptively within the cultural constraints of His day and His selection of the twelve is one occasion where it seems that He did so, likely for the reasons listed above. Either way, His selection of the twelve said nothing about the inherent capacity of females and their ability to exercise spiritual authority in His church any more than choosing twelve *Jewish* men speaks to the inherent leadership capacity of Gentiles. We can confidently conclude this is the case from the approach Christ took to other women in His ministry already outlined in this chapter.

The Rest of The New Testament

The influence of Jesus' approach to women continued in the history of the early church. Examples of women serving, leading and teaching abound in the book of Acts and throughout the various epistles. In what follows we will highlight a few of the most notable examples.

In the book of Acts we meet several prominent female leaders in the early church. Priscilla and Aquila—a married couple with whom Paul briefly travelled, lived and worked[8] —taught the male leader Apollos.[9] It is often pointed out that Priscilla is repeatedly named first. Kate Cooper, Professor of Ancient History at the University of Manchester, notes that, "Ancient writers often referred to a married couple by the man's name only, so the choice to name Priscilla, and to put her name first, is significant."[10] The unconventional nature of her being mentioned first, given their cultural context, may very well point to the fact that she was the primary teacher of the husband/wife team. As another scholar writes,

> It is hard to avoid the conclusion that within this husband and wife team it was Priscilla who was the more noticeable partner and whose ministry was particularly important for the growth of

---

8 Acts 18:2-3
9 Acts 18:26
10 Cooper, 6.

> the church. That a Jewish woman should be recorded as taking the lead in giving religious instruction to the Jewish teacher Apollos, 'an eloquent man, well-versed in the Scriptures' is, by contemporary Jewish standards, quite astounding—and Paul's evident approval of her activity is very hard to square with the traditional interpretation of 1 Timothy 2:11-12 as forbidding any woman ever to teach or have authority over a man! [11] [12]

Elsewhere in the book of Acts, Luke recounts his and Paul's introduction to Lydia, a Gentile woman whom they met upon their arrival in Greece:

> On the Sabbath we went outside the city gate to the river, where we expected to find a place of prayer. We sat down and began to speak to the women who had gathered there. One of those listening was a woman from the city of Thyatira named Lydia, a dealer in purple cloth. She was a worshiper of God. The Lord opened her heart to respond to Paul's message. When she and the members of her household were baptized, she invited us to

---

11 R.T. France, *Women in the Church's Ministry* (Grand Rapids, MI: Eerdmans, 1995), 80.

12 "The case of Priscilla is debated, but it seems specious and unreasonable to argue that hers was not legitimate teaching because she instructed Apollos in her home and not in a church service or because she is said to have "explained" the"way of God" rather than to have "taught" the "Scriptures" (Acts 18:26). After all, the church *met* in her home (Rom 16:3-5), and in any case, how does one explain something without teaching? "The way of God" was a recognizable phrase for God's truth and the gospel in those early days when the New Testament Scriptures were not yet completed. Walter L. Liefeld, "The Nature of Authority in the New Testament." Editors Robert W. Pierce & Rebecca Merrill Groothuis, *Discovering Biblical Equality: Complementarity without Hierarchy* (Downers Grove, Ill: Intervarsity Press, 2004), 265.

> her home. 'If you consider me a believer in the Lord,' she said, 'come and stay at my house.' And she persuaded us.[13]

Thus, Lydia became the first convert to Christianity in Europe. And it was with Lydia and this group of women who gathered for prayer on a riverbank that Paul's mission to Greece—and ultimately the history of Christianity in Europe—found its first footing.[14]

In the book of Romans we find more evidence of women who played an important role in the life of the church. In Romans 16:7, Junia is said to be "prominent among the apostles," a statement from which one should conclude that she played a prominent teaching and leadership role in the Christian community—a role that was celebrated by the apostle Paul. The gender of Junia is sometimes debated, but it would seem as though any doubt as to whether the name is female or male is usually motivated by a theological agenda, rather than textual or contextual considerations. In the words of R.T. France, "No other instance of the masculine name Junias is known [in the surrounding centuries], and there seems little doubt that it would not have been suggested here but for the unwillingness of some in the Western church to accept that a woman could be described as prominent among the apostles."[15]

The closing chapter of Paul's letter to the Romans mentions a number of other female leaders as being co-workers in their own

---

13 Acts 16:13-15

14 Cooper, 14-15.

15 R.T. France, *Women in the Church's Ministry* (Grand Rapids, MI: Eerdmans, 1995), This reluctance has also led to a debate around translations, which we don't have room to dive into here.

right, rather than alongside their husbands.[16] This includes the naming of specific women: Phoebe, Mary, Tryphena, Tryphosa, Persis, and Julia.[17]

In fact, it was one of these women, Phoebe, who carried and delivered this very letter of Paul's to the Roman church. The apostle Paul calls her a deaconess and, in doing so, gives her a glowing endorsement. He writes, "I commend to you our sister Phoebe, a servant (*diakonon* = deaconess) of the church in Cenchrea. I ask you to receive her in the Lord in a way worthy of the saints and to give her any help she may need from you, for she has been a great help to many people, including me" (Romans 16:1-3). It is worth noting that the bearer of the letter would be tasked with reading it to the gathered congregation, communicating with the proper emphasis and inflection, and would often have been coached by the sender of the letter itself. More than that, Phoebe would have had the responsibility of commentating on the meaning of Paul's instructions and answering any questions the people might have had, which makes sense in light of the fact that she was the one in contact with the writer of the letter, as well as being the one entrusted with its delivery to the church in Rome. Likely the most influential epistle the Apostle Paul ever wrote was first interpreted and expounded by a woman to the benefit and blessing of the church in Rome.

Other significant co-workers of Paul included two prominent female leaders in the Philippian congregation. Euodia and Syntyche were female leaders in the congregation at Philippi whom the apostle Paul considered co-laborers in the Gospel.[18]

---

16 Cooper, 8.
17 Romans 16:1,6,12,15.
18 Philippians 4:2

Paul describes them with the same phrase he uses for many of the male leaders who served alongside him; yet another example of him treating female leaders as equal in Christ.

Female Prophets in The New Testament

In the New Testament we encounter plenty of evidence that women were prophesying in the church. Anna prophecies about Christ, instructing His parents about the Messianic identity of their son,[19] a teaching which is recorded in scripture and, therefore, has authority over all who read it.[20] Philip's four daughters possessed the gift of prophecy[21] and in the Corinthian church women were prophesying in the congregation (1 Corinthians 11:5). The apostle Paul writes, "And every woman who prays or prophesies with her head uncovered dishonours her head..." Leaving the matter of head covers to one side, this instruction clearly assumes that women are both praying and prophesying publicly when the church is gathered. The prophetic gift did involve spontaneous sharing and exhortation, but it also had an instructive element for the church community, whether it be boldly proclaiming the word of God into a certain circumstance or foretelling the future.

The apostle Paul in the same letter to the Corithians, while sorting out the disorderly worship in the church, writes, "Two or three prophets should speak, one at a time, and the others should weigh what is being said... For you can all prophesy in turn so that everyone may be instructed and encouraged" (1 Corinthians 14:29,31).

---

19 Luke 2:36-38
20 Ibid, 256.
21 Acts 21:8-9; see also Acts 2:16-18

Paul tells us that:

1. Women were prophesying in the Corinthian congregation to men and women (1 Corinthians 11:5).

2. Prophecy involved instruction and encouragement (1 Corinthians 14:29,31).

3. Therefore, women were instructing men and women in the Corinthian congregation.

When the implications of this sink in we should be led to conclude that women were exercising a degree of spiritual authority in proclaiming God's word to their hearers.

All of the New Testament data presented in this chapter makes it clear that women were engaged in all different kinds of ministry, including teaching. This evidence makes it all the more odd that in two notable places in his letters Paul seems to silence women and severely restrict their ability to teach and lead in the church. As we close this chapter and head into the next two chapters which will explore the two most controversial texts in this conversation, we will be confronted with a decision:

Will we interpret all of the above information in light of two seemingly more restrictive passages in Paul's letters? Or will we interpret these seemingly more prohibitive passages in light of both their original context and the abundance of New Testament evidence, including: women disciples, women missionaries, women evangelists, women prophets, women preachers, women leaders and women apostles? We believe that we should do the latter rather than the former, especially when these two particular passages can be understood in multiple ways without doing violence to the text and without reigning in the freedom for women in ministry that otherwise bursts through the pages of the New Testament.

CHAPTER 3
CHAOS IN CORINTH AND THE SILENCING OF WOMEN[1]

.... Elita & Chris

When my (Chris's) daughter was five years old I took her shopping. I was looking for a new shirt. When I try on shirts I have a tendency to gesture as though I am preaching to check for fit.

---

1 In this chapter we don't mention 1 Corinthians 11:2-16. It is a strange passage that is difficult to understand. Paul does refer to the creation story and he does mention issues of headship and authority. He also makes some very strong egalitarian claims (vs. 11, 12). Nevertheless, in my opinion this text is not strictly relevant to the case being argued for in this book, so we have left it to the Q and R section at the end. I only note the salient fact that women are prophesying in the Corinthian church. The purpose of prophecy is to strengthen, encourage, instruct and comfort the church, which, in the eyes of many, is also the purpose of a sermon. In referencing women prophesying, this passage lends strong credibility to the interpretation we give of 1 Corinthians 14 in this book.

My daughter, who was in the change room with me, noticed me doing this and exclaimed,

"You're preaching!"

I responded, "Yeah, I'm pretending. Are you going to preach too?"

Without skipping a beat she replied, "No, I can't preach. I'm not a boy."

No one had told her that, but she still said it. Was she right or wrong? Would the apostle Paul agree with her five-year old heart or not? These are the questions—questions that don't live only in theory, but in the hearts of little girls wondering what is possible and what is not.

Women Should Remain Silent?

In 1 Corinthians 14:34-35 Paul states, "Women should remain silent in the churches. They are not allowed to speak, but must be in submission, as the Law says. If they want to inquire about something, they should ask their own husbands at home; for it is disgraceful for a woman to speak in church." In this short passage Paul seems to have turned from a liberator of women in ministry to an oppressor, from a champion of women in the church to a cantankerous autocrat who is intent on silencing female voices. How are we to understand Paul's instruction here?

The broader context of this instruction is disorderly worship in the church—context which helps us discern what Paul means here. Here's what we already know: it can't mean that women must always be silent. We have seen in 1 Corinthians 11 that Paul acknowledged the prophesying of women. The purpose of prophecy was to publicly instruct and encourage all who were present. And it is hard to prophecy and pray publicly without speaking! This means that the "plain meaning" of the text in question can't be the right one and we will need to dig a little deeper. This deserves to be spelled out as clearly as possible.

1. The plain meaning of, "Women should remain silent in churches. They should not be allowed to speak," is that women should not talk in churches.

2. But elsewhere, Paul encourages women to speak in churches, including 1 Corinthians 11.

3. Therefore, unless we intend to accuse the apostle Paul of contradicting himself within the span of three short chapters, the plain meaning of 1 Corinthians 14 cannot be the right one. It must be a certain type of "speaking" that is being prohibited.

So what type of speaking is being highlighted in this passage?

Many scholars think it likely that the women in the Corinthian church had been interrupting the teacher during the public worship, asking questions about what was being taught, and that Paul was instructing them to refrain from doing this, instead encouraging them to speak with their husbands at home.[2] Their willingness to be disruptive in this manner was shameful, to use Paul's word. It may have been the result of cultural factors like a lack of theological education or a lack of experience in public settings—a residual reflection of the patriarchal nature of that day

2 For example, see John Temple Bristow, *What Paul Really Said About Women* (New York, NY: HarperCollins Publishing, 1991).

and the homebound reality of many women. John Stackhouse does well in summarizing this view when he writes,

> Women in this culture, as in most cultures in the history of the world, generally were not educated beyond the domestic arts. Furthermore, they were not socialized into the discourse of formal, public learning. So, in the enthusiasm of their Christian liberty, in the excitement of the freedom found in their full acceptance into the church alongside men, it appears that some women would disrupt meetings with inappropriate questions and other unedifying talk.[3]

Kari Torjesen Malcolm served as a missionary in China like her parents before her. She has fascinating insight to offer on this passage:

> My mother used to compare the situation in Corinth to the one she and my father faced in northern China. Back in the 1920's when they were first to bring God's message to that forgotten area, they found women with bound feet who seldom left their homes and who, unlike the men, had never in their whole lives attended a public meeting or a class. They had never been told as little girls, 'Now you must sit still and listen to the teacher.' Their only concept of an assembly was a family feast where everyone talked at once. When these women came to my parents' church and gathered on the women's side of the sanctuary, they thought this was a chance to catch up on the news with their neighbours and to ask questions about the story of Jesus

---

3 John G. Stackhouse Jr., *Partners In Christ: A Conservative Case for Egalitarianism* (Downers Grove, Ill: InterVarsity Press, 2015), 67.

> they were hearing. Needless to say, along with babies crying and toddlers running about, the women's section got rather noisy! Add to that the temptation for the women to shout questions to their husbands across the aisle, and you can imagine the chaos. As my mother patiently tried to tell the women that they should listen first and chitchat or ask questions later, she would mutter under her breath, 'Just like Corinthian; it just couldn't be more like Corinth.[4]

Such an interpretation fits into the larger context of disorderly and chaotic worship, and may also allow us to solve a riddle that has puzzled many commentators regarding the precise nature of the law to which Paul is referring.

Normally when Paul speaks of the law he does so in reference to the Old Testament law. This has puzzled commentators because in the Pentateuch there is neither a specific command that would silence women in the congregation, nor one that refers specifically to the submission of women in the religious community. Some scholars have suggested that Paul is referring to an unknown oral tradition, but evidence for this is inconclusive. What some commentators have then pointed out is that in Galatians 5:14, Paul also writes about the law of love. It is feasible, therefore, that in this text he is referring to the law of love, which he also mentions in 1 Corinthians 13 when sorting out the abuse of spiritual gifts. The meaning could then be interpreted: In accordance with the law of love, submit to your other brothers and sisters, seeking to benefit from the corporate teaching of

---

4 Kari Torjesen Malcolm, *Women at the Crossroads* (Downers Grove, Ill: InterVarsity, 1982), 73-74.

God's word by remaining silent—ask your questions at home.[5]

Though the interpretation argued for above should be held tentatively, it remains a very probable understanding of what was going on in Corinth. As mentioned earlier, it has the added benefit of avoiding a scenario where the apostle Paul blatantly contradicts himself within the span of just three chapters by first encouraging women to prophesy in chapter 11 and then silencing them in chapter 14. Either way, it should be clear that this passage would not forbid the preaching and teaching ministry of educated and godly women in today's church.

---

5 Ibid, 65. This understanding of Paul's reference to the law is, of course, contested. Many have a tendency to root Paul's command in the creation order and the equal value but distinct roles that men and women are intended to fill. For an example of this approach see, Craig Bloomberg, *The NIV Application Commentary: 1 Corinthians* (Grand Rapids, MI: Zondervan Publishing, 1994).

CHAPTER 4
TROUBLE IN EPHESUS

.... Elita & Chris

My (Chris') wife recently saw a meme that said, "I'm giving up drinking for a month. No, wait... I mean... I'm giving up. Drinking for a month." This is how I (Chris) sometimes feel when engaging this debate, but that is beside the point. The reason I mention it is this: notice that both sentences use the same exact words, but have two radically different meanings. The only difference is one little period.

Just as punctuation matters when trying to determine meaning, so does the surrounding context of a word or statement. Whereas the real estate mantra might be, "Location, location, location," the mantra of proper biblical interpretation could be, "Context, context, context." To take a statement out of context can radically alter its meaning, leading to confusion and wrong judgments.

Context matters.

This is crucial to keep in mind as we approach the most important, controversial passage in the debate regarding women in ministry.

1 Timothy 2:11-14

In 1 Timothy 2:11-14 the apostle Paul writes,

> A woman should learn in quietness and full submission. I do not permit a woman to teach or have authority over a man; she must be silent. For Adam was formed first, then Eve. And Adam was not the one deceived; it was the woman who was deceived and became a sinner. But women will be saved through child bearing—if they continue in faith, love and holiness with propriety.

This is the most frequently used passage used to forbid women from preaching and teaching in the church when men are present. It is not going too far to say that this might be the key text in the entire debate. Before we embrace what some would feel is an obvious conclusion—that Paul is prohibiting women from teaching and exercising a form of leadership/authority over men—we need to slow down a bit. Remember that in 1 Corinthians 14 the plain reading of the text would silence women from ever speaking in the church—a position that, thankfully, very few hold. So when we come to this passage we shouldn't immediately jump to any conclusions either. Instead, let us dig a little deeper into the actual *meaning* of his instructions. To discover this, we will need to spend time delving into the surrounding context of the passage.

Context

The apostle Paul's instruction here is once again given within the context of disorderly worship. Though he begins by urging women to learn "in quietness and full submission," this is not actually as controversial as it first appears. Paul's focus is on submission to the word of God and the authority of scripture, and the quietness he advocates for is for the purpose of active listening. This is, of course, how the entire church, male and female, should listen to the word of God: in submission to scripture's authority with attentive hearts and minds.[1] It is also worth pausing to recognize that Paul starts by saying, "A woman *should* learn...",[2] a remarkable fact in and of itself. Paul is encouraging the women to learn the scripture; he is instructing the women to be good theologians who can correctly handle the word of truth. Sadly, as we've already mentioned, in Jewish culture it was common not to allow women to sit in the position of a disciple. Great pains were taken to instruct Jewish boys in the Torah, but the girls were usually excluded after the age of 12. Although that was the culture Paul grew up in, here we see that his commendation to have the women learn and grow in their understanding

---

1 "An additional factor in the interpretation of the quietness and submission of women in learning is that this attitude was also expected of male students studying under a rabbi, who, after ordination, would be both teaching and exercising authority." Walter L. Liefeld, *1 & 2 Timothy/Titus: The NIV Application Commentary* (Grand Rapids, MI: Zondervan, 1999), 97.

2 Emphasis added

of God's word was actually moving the culture forward in a more equitable direction. The apostle Paul is following in the footsteps of his Lord Jesus, who encouraged women to be His disciples and sit at His feet to learn.[3]

In the next verse, however, matters get a little more complex: "I do not permit a woman to teach or exercise authority over a man." On the surface, this statement appears to clearly forbid a woman from speaking when the church is gathered. Yet, as we have seen earlier, there are many other situations where the scripture does not forbid women to teach men. As good interpreters of scripture this should lead us to believe that Paul *must be referring to a specific kind of teaching*.[4] In fact, no matter what

---

3 Luke 10:38-42

4 The readers should be made aware of the fact that there are many different interpretations of this passage amongst egalitarians and complementarians. One example would be John Dickson and his book, *Hearing Her Voice*. In 1 Timothy 2 the NIV has, "I do not permit a woman to teach or to have authority over a man." I think this is the best translation but the construction in Greek can be translated slightly differently. It can be referring to teaching and authority as separate issues, or to a type of authoritative teaching. Dickson argues that Paul is using the words "authoritative teaching" in a very specific sense. He is referring to the passing on of the apostolic tradition in a time period when a lot of Jesus' teachings were not yet written down and their transmission and preservation was totally dependent on the accurate reportage of the apostles who, for the most part, were men. In his own words, "For Paul, 'teaching' (in the technical sense) involved carefully preserving and laying down for the congregation the traditions handed on by the apostles. In the period before the texts of the New Testament were readily available, a church's only access to the range of things apostles had said about Jesus and his demands was through a teacher, the one entrusted with the 'apostolic deposit'." Dickson, John, *Hearing Her Voice* (Grand Rapids, MI: Zondervan Publishing, 2012), 29. He then argues that when we refer to preaching and teaching in the modern church we are talking about the parsing of an authoritative text and an exhortation based on the text, not teaching in the technical sense used by Paul. Therefore, 1 Timothy 2 should not be used to forbid women from teaching or preaching in the church.

position you hold in this debate, everyone believes that Paul is referring to a certain type of teaching. For example, no one thinks that Paul is forbidding women from teaching other women, or from women teaching children or, perhaps, even youth. So, what type of teaching is Paul prohibiting women to do?

He doesn't explicitly tell us.

To answer that question we need to go beyond the plain words of this scripture and infer what type of instruction he is putting a lid on based on evidence both from the immediate context of the passage and from throughout his letter to Timothy.

First, let's turn to the actual letter of 1 Timothy and the issue of false teaching.

Context, Context, Context

In this section we will investigate the clues littered throughout Paul's letter that provide a broader picture of what is taking place in the church, specifically related to false teaching. Here are some significant texts:

> Stay there in Ephesus so that you may command certain people not to teach false doctrines any longer or to devote themselves to myths and endless genealogies. Such things promote controversial speculations rather than advancing God's work—which is by faith.
>
> 1 Timothy 1:3-5

Paul also tells Timothy to keep "holding on to faith and a good conscience. Some have rejected these and so have shipwrecked their faith. Among them are Hymenaeus and Alexander, whom

I have handed over to Satan to be taught not to blaspheme" (1 Timothy 1:19,20). In chapter 4 of the letter we get a window into some of the content being taught by the false teachers:

> The Spirit clearly says that in later times some will abandon the faith and follow deceiving spirits and things taught by demons. Such teachings come through hypocritical liars, whose consciences have been seared as with a hot iron. They forbid people to marry and order them to abstain from certain foods, which God created to be received with thanksgiving by those who know the truth.
>
> 1 Timothy 4:1-4

This type of textual evidence makes it clear that the apostle Paul's foremost concern is regarding false teaching that is taking place in the church. In fact, one could argue that false teaching is the primary reason he wrote this epistle to the church in Ephesus—it consumes 35 percent of Paul's explicit attention in this letter.[5] It is poor exegesis to not read 1 Timothy against the backdrop of false teaching. There is also no other epistle that addresses women so frequently. It shouldn't, therefore, be a

---

5 At the end of chapter one, Paul names two false teachers who have shipwrecked their faith, "Hymenaeus and Alexander, whom I have handed over to Satan to be taught not to blaspheme" (1 Tim. 1:20). It is unclear why Paul chooses to mention these two men in particular; perhaps it was because they were very influential, or the example of their apostasy was well known. Either way we need not assume that because he mentions two men by name that it was only these men who were teaching false doctrine. In fact, we should conclude the exact opposite given that Paul says that some have shipwrecked their faith, *including* Hymenaeus and Alexander, clearly implying that these men were prominent members of a larger group of unnamed individuals. Again, the undeniable fact is that false teaching is a prevalent problem in the Ephesian church.

stretch for the careful reader to make a connection between both false teaching and the activity of women in the Ephesian church.

What type of teaching, then, is Paul forbidding women to engage in at the church in Ephesus? Given the context, it is very likely that Paul's prohibition of women teaching in the Ephesian church is due to both the lack of *theological* education possessed by women in the congregation and the prevalence of false teaching. And, more than just the false teaching, we suggest that Paul's restrictive statement must also be understood as addressing the aggressive or domineering fashion in which women in the congregation were approaching the whole matter of public instruction—a conclusion we argue for below.

What Does Authority Mean?

"I do not permit a woman to teach or to have authority over a man; she must be silent" (1 Timothy 2:12). Here Paul also seems to prevent a woman from exercising authority over a man. Remember our repeated caution about the importance of context. It comes into play again here. We have probably all noticed how the same word can have a different meaning depending on context or culture or time in history. This is called the semantic range of a word. A classic example would be the word "football". Depending on the country you are in, the word football describes substantially different sports: soccer in the UK, the NFL in America and Aussie rules in Australia. The same word can be used with different meanings.

So what about the word "authority"? What does Paul mean when he writes that he doesn't permit a woman to exercise authority over a man? Elsewhere he writes that a wife has authority over her husband's body just as he has authority over hers (1 Corinthians 7:4). So what type of authority is he referring to here? The authority that a husband and wife share with one another? The authority that comes with functioning as a leader? Is he referring to any use of authority, a specific type of authority or an abusive use of authority?

Interestingly, the Greek word *authentein,* translated as "authority" in this passage, appears nowhere else in the New Testament. To determine how the word was being used during that time period one has to go outside of the New Testament. The scholar Linda L. Belleville, in her thorough survey of the word's usage, proves decisively that the semantic range of this word is vast when one factors in its usage in extra-biblical literature. *Authentein* is used to mean murderer, sponsor, perpetrator, originator or the mastermind of a crime or an act of violence.[6] For example, she points out that the word *authentein* appears in the Wisdom of Solomon, an intertestamental piece of Jewish literature, where it is used to describe the act of murder: "Those who lived long ago in your holy land, you hated for their detestable practices...parents who murdered (authentas) helpless lives." In an ancient commentary on Aeschylus, the verb is again used to express the committing of a murder. N.T. Wright understands the word to convey the meaning of "being bossy" or "seizing control".[7] The scholar Kenneth Bailey has pointed out to fellow scholars that ancient Syriac and Arabic versions of 1 Timothy

---

6 Editor, James R. Beck, *Two Views of Women in Ministry* (Grand Rapids, MI: Zondervan Academic, 2005).
7 Ibid, 70.

understand the verb to mean "bullying" or "domineering".[8] Here is what is crucial to note: there are *no positive meanings* ascribed to the word until after the 2nd century AD, and most appear in the 3rd and 4th century. Not only that, there were plenty of other words Paul could have chosen to clearly communicate the idea of a proper and legitimate use of authority. For example, the Greek word *exousia*, which is most frequently used in the New Testament to refer to Jesus' authority. Instead the word Paul used was routinely employed to describe an abusive form of authority that was domineering, usurping, bullying or acting violently.[9] Therefore, when Paul writes that he doesn't permit a woman to exercise authority over a man it is far more likely he is referring to an idea like getting one's way or dominating another person. The meaning would be, "I don't permit a woman to teach in a way that dominates men or to gain mastery over men." As another scholar writes:

> The women at Ephesus (perhaps encouraged by false teachers) were trying to gain an advantage over the men by teaching in a dictatorial fashion. The men in response became angry and

---

8 R.T. France, *Women in the Church's Ministry: A Test Case for Biblical Interpretation* (Grand Rapids, MI: William B. Eerdmans Publishing Company, 1995), 65.

9 This is still debated in scholarly literature. However, R.T. France might be on point when he writes, "Here is another debate which is not likely to be settled definitively, given the scarcity of the verb. Certainly Paul forbids a woman to exercise authority over a man (or her husband), but the question whether he refers to any authority at all, or more specifically to a misused, usurped authority, remains unresolved. If he intended to say that no woman may ever be in a position where she has authority over a man, he has chosen an unnecessarily obscure way to say it!" R.T. France, *Women in the Church's Ministry: A Test Case for Biblical Interpretation* (Grand Rapids, MI: William B. Eerdmans Publishing Company, 1995).

> disputed what the women were doing. This interpretation fits the broader context of 1 Timothy 2:8-15, where Paul aims to correct inappropriate behaviour on the part of both men and women.[10]

Now, the most likely explanation for why the women in Ephesus were acting in this manner is the influence of the cult of Artemis, a cult in which the female was exalted and viewed as far superior to the male.

The Cult of Artemis

The main religion in Ephesus, boasting the largest temple and most significant shrine, was the cult of Artemis. It took 120 years to build the temple and it loomed over everything in the city. It was the greatest of the Seven Wonders of the ancient world. The enormous, extravagant image of Artemis would have impressed itself on the religious consciousness of every resident living in 1st century Ephesus. Think of Paul's own experience at Ephesus: he witnessed a citywide riot that ended up at the stadium with a crowd of thousands chanting, "Great is Artemis of Ephesus" for over two hours—a riot that was only quieted down when the city clerk said, "Men of Ephesus, doesn't all the world know that the city of Ephesus is the guardian of the temple of the great Artemis and of her image, which fell from heaven? Therefore, since these facts are undeniable, you ought to be quiet and not do anything rash" (Acts 19:35-36). This event not only sheds a lot of light on the culture in Ephesus, we are sure it is an experience that the

---

10 Editor, James R. Beck, *Two Views of Women in Ministry* (Grand Rapids, MI: Zondervan Academic, 2005), 89.

Apostle Paul never forgot!

The worship of Artemis—or Diana, to the Romans—was a female-only cult with a priesthood composed solely of women. I (Chris) have in front of me a book by Pausanias, a 2nd century author, called *Guide to Greece*, in which he spends time outlining the female dominance inherent in this cult. Greeks believed that Artemis was the offspring of Zeus and Leto. Artemis had forsaken the affection and advances of the male gods and, instead, pursued the affection and company of a human consort named Leimon. The popular belief was that Artemis, in flouting the affection of the male gods, was superior—a superiority she shared with all her female adherents and priestesses.

So, when modern-day scholars like N.T. Wright claim that in the temple of Artemis the women "ruled the show and kept the men in their place", they are not pulling such a statement out of thin air.[11] Given the enormous religious influence of Artemis and given that this was the situation between men and women in the cult of Artemis, it is not hard to imagine that this approach to spiritual authority was creeping into the church in Ephesus and impacting the behaviour of the women who had converted out of a pagan background.

Taking all of this evidence into account, it seems very reasonable to conclude that Paul may be addressing a unique circumstance rooted in the cultural situation facing the Ephesian church. A circumstance involving a lack of theological education amongst the women, false teaching and an inappropriate expression of authority which was aggressive and domineering—one belonging more in the Temple of Artemis than in the temple of

---

11 N.T. Wright, *Paul For Everyone: The Pastoral Letters: 1 and 2 Timothy* (Downers Grove, Ill: Intervarsity Press, 2009), 60. Kindle Edition.

the living God, the church of Christ. On the positive, side Paul was claiming, like Jesus in Luke 10, that women must have the space to study and learn—not in order that they may muscle in and take over the leadership as in the Artemis cult, but so that men and women alike can develop whatever gifts of learning, teaching and leadership God is giving them.

Some might express concern that this understanding of the text limits its impact to a 1st century setting. It is, however, important to note for the contemporary reader that these unique circumstances are not entirely time-bound or limited strictly to a 1st century setting. We see that both false teaching and an inappropriate expression of authority are still practiced today and are, therefore, still censored by Paul's instructions to the church in Ephesus, making this scripture perennially relevant to the modern church.

What about Paul's Reference to Adam and Eve?

For those who hold to a position that restricts the ability of women to preach, teach or lead the gathered people of God, the above contextual and cultural considerations remain unconvincing for a number of reasons. The primary cause for such resistance, as it pertains to this passage, is the fact that Paul mentions the story of Adam and Eve in verses 13-15: "For Adam was formed first, then Eve. And Adam was not the one deceived; it was the woman who was deceived and became a sinner." Many theologians in the above camp believe that Paul is grounding his instruction in a "creation principle" rooted in the Genesis narrative, the intrinsic make-up of men and women and the roles that God intends us to fulfill at home and in the church.

In a short book entitled, *On Church Leadership*, one well-known pastor writes that "God made the man first, which established him as the leader responsible for the rest of creation in the same way that a firstborn son was responsible for his siblings throughout the Old Testament." He goes on to claim that "God permitted the man to name the woman and in that act exercise authority over her." When it comes to 1 Timothy 2 he concludes that Paul

> ...argues against female elders-pastors from the Genesis account of creation. Whereas Paul's declaration that men should be pastors because God made them first may sound odd to us, it did make perfect sense to his original audience, who understood that throughout the Old Testament the firstborn was a position of extra responsibility in the family. Since God intentionally made man first, Paul reasons, then men are expected to take primary responsibility for the leadership of the church.[12]

This line of thought is often referred to as the creation principle. But is the exegesis sound? First, all of the above conclusions, though stated confidently, represent inferences as to what the scripture must mean, not what the text "clearly" teaches. For example, the author writes that in the garden, "God permitted the man to name the woman and in that act exercise authority over her." This argument is unpersuasive for a multitude of reasons. Iain Provan, an expert in the Old Testament, points out that,

> Some believe that the naming of the female by the male in Genesis 2:23 indicates his claim to authority over her. However, although naming is indeed often carried out in the Old

12 Mark Driscoll, *On Church Leadership* (Wheaton, Ill: Crossway, 2008), 36,42.

> Testament by those who have authority over others (e.g., parents), it cannot be demonstrated that the act of naming in itself involves the assertion of authority. A strong example that points in the opposite direction is Hagar's naming of God in Genesis 16:13. In Genesis 2:23 itself, the naming certainly carries no connotation of a claim to authority. The reverse is in fact true. First of all, the man names not only the woman but also himself. Does this imply that the male is taking authority over himself?... The names do not imply any kind of hierarchy.[13]

Moreover, though the firstborn throughout the Old Testament does often assume a position of extra responsibility, this practice is nowhere God-ordained but, instead, reflects the customs of the day. In fact, God constantly subverts the order in the family by choosing the youngest over the oldest. We see this throughout the book of Genesis.

Lastly, the above meaning being *read into* Paul's use of the creation story by those who refer to it as a creation principle involves a strange and awkward leap of logic. As two scholars quip, "What difference does it make that Adam came before Eve? Wouldn't this same logic require that the animals have authority over humans, since they were created before us?"[14]

R.T. France is perhaps the most incisive when dismantling the logic behind this reading of 1 Timothy 2:13-15:

---

13 Iain Provan, *Seriously Dangerous Religion*, 91. It is true that in Genesis 3 Adam again names the woman Eve. But it must also be noted that Adam properly names the woman after the fall, so such an act does not likely represent God's ideal.

14 Gregory A. Boyd & Paul R. Eddy, *Across the Spectrum: Understanding Issues in Evangelical Theology* (Grand Rapids, MI: Baker Academic, 2009), 259.

> If the logic is simply that the first to be created must necessarily be superior, one might wonder why human beings are not subject to the rest of the animal creation. If it is that the woman was responsible for the entry of sin and therefore women are inevitably the source of sin and false teaching, why does Paul argue in Romans 5 that sin came through the transgression of Adam, with no mention of Eve? If he is arguing that women cannot be trusted with authority because Eve's example shows that they are inherently more gullible (a generalization which is not always verified by experience!), in what sense is this a creation principle? (It might better be called a fall principle, and that would raise interesting questions about its validity in the era of redemption!)[15]

After taking the above points into consideration, it should be clear that the attempt to restrict a woman from preaching or teaching based on a creation principle, the intrinsic differences between men and women or some kind of priority of creation, is far from convincing.

Instead, we suggest an interpretation which connects to the issues of women learning theology, false teaching and a vulnerability to false doctrine—issues which are highlighted throughout the rest of the letter. Here is what we think Paul is doing when he quotes the creation story. Rather than appealing to some sort of creation principle, Paul is referencing Adam and Eve as an illustration to make an important point. In being formed first, Adam possessed information which Eve did not have firsthand access to, making it necessary for her to be instructed. Without

---

15 R.T. France, *Women in the Church's Ministry* (Grand Rapids, MI: Eerdmans, 1995), 67.

this guidance, she would be extremely vulnerable to Satan's false teaching or mishandling of God's word. With this in mind, we believe that Paul is referencing the creation story to address the issue of vulnerability to false teaching. As we have noted, many of the women in Ephesus, though possibly educated in other areas, lacked theological education. Jewish women would not have received the same instruction in the Torah as Jewish men, and Roman women would have no understanding of scripture at all. They needed to receive instruction so they wouldn't be deceived like Eve was and propagate false doctrine. N.T. Wright suggests that Paul is concerned with the women being taught theology precisely because apart from such instruction they will, like Eve, be prone to deception.[16] In the words of another scholar, "The story of Adam and Eve shows how important it is to faithfully teach others so that no one falls into deception. That is why Paul's one command in this chapter was: the woman must learn."[17]

There are two other arguments strongly in favour of the position presented above. First, it reflects a common rabbinic understanding of what happened in the garden (recalling that the Apostle Paul was trained as a rabbi).

> According to this tradition, Adam was at fault for not properly instructing Eve about the dangers and consequences of eating from the forbidden tree. Adam had been created first and had received instructions directly from God. Eve had been created second and was dependent on Adam for this information. This

---

16 N.T. Wright, *Paul For Everyone: The Pastoral Letters: 1 and 2 Timothy* (Downers Grove, Ill: Intervarsity Press, 2009), 60. Kindle Edition.
17 Loren Cunningham & David Joel Hamilton, *Why Not Women?* (Seattle, WA: YWAM Publishing, 2000), 223.

is why she was more vulnerable and also why Adam bore the brunt of responsibility for the fall.[18] [19]

Second, it aligns with how Paul uses the creation story elsewhere in his writings:

> I promised you to one husband, to Christ, so that I might present you as a pure virgin to him. But I am afraid that just as Eve was deceived by the serpent's cunning, your minds may somehow be led astray from your sincere and pure devotion to Christ. For if someone comes to you and preaches a Jesus other than the Jesus we preached, or if you receive a different spirit from the Spirit you received, or a different gospel from the one you accepted, you put up with it easily enough.
>
> 2 Corinthians 11:2-4

Here Paul clearly highlights the example of Eve and the creation story to address vulnerability to false teaching and the

---

18 Gregory A. Boyd & Paul R. Eddy, *Across the Spectrum: Understanding Issues in Evangelical Theology* (Grand Rapids, MI: Baker Academic, 2009), 259.

19 David Joel Hamilton and Loren Cunningham in their book *Why Not Women?* see things in a similar light, but with a few interesting differences. These authors argue that Paul is only referring to one woman in the congregation. In their view Paul is actually not silencing women in general, but one woman in the congregation who is teaching false doctrine. This allows them to draw a tidy parallel between Eve and this false teacher. "Paul reminds Timothy that Adam sinned with his eyes open, but Eve did so because she was deceived. Paul held Adam more accountable for his sin because Adam wasn't deceived when he decided to disobey God. However, Eve's sin was the fruit, not of knowing disobedience but of deception. One of the major themes of this entire passage was stopping the deception in the Ephesian church. Eve was deceived, and so was this woman who was to be silenced. Both were acting on false beliefs. What these two women had in common was they both had believed a lie. As a result, they both had sinned."

possibility of deception. This gives us confidence that, rather than appealing to some type of creation principle and the inherited differences between men and women, Paul is using the story of Eve in 1 Timothy 2 as an illustration to point out that the women need to be taught theology so that they are not vulnerable to false teaching.

If the above scenario is the case, and there are good reasons to think it is, it should be clear that Paul's prohibition in Ephesus and his reference of the creation story would not constitute a blanket ban on all educated, theologically informed women teaching, for all time, and in all places where the people of God gathered. Not only that, the New Testament's picture of women in ministry is more in sync with an understanding of 1 Timothy 2 that forbids women from teaching false doctrine—or teaching in a way that claimed an undue, abusive authority over men—rather than a blanket-ban on the body of Christ benefitting from called, competent, charismatic women teachers when the whole church gathers today.

Saved Through Childbearing?

One confusing matter remains that reiterates the importance of context: What does Paul mean when he says that "women will be saved through childbearing"? Without understanding context the plain words would lead us to believe that salvation comes through childbearing—an interpretation that would leave us with devastating theological implications to the doctrine of salvation by grace alone, as well as disheartening practical implications for men and women without children. Paul's comment seems both strange and contrary to salvation by grace alone, through faith alone, in the finished work of Christ alone. Once again, when seeking to understand this teaching we are confronted with various explanations that are reliant on context. It could be that Paul is again countering the influence of Artemis who was looked upon as the protector of women and the goddess of fertility. In 1st century Ephesus women turned to Artemis for safe travel through the childbearing process. With this in mind, Paul would be assuring the women in the church that, in rejecting a false god, they are still under the protection of the true and living God who will save them and take care of them through the travails of childbirth.[20] This explanation not only makes sense of an otherwise confusing text, it also ties together the entire thread of Paul's instructions very nicely.

We would be remiss, however, if we didn't mention one other possible solution: the original language may be a factor in properly understanding Paul's words. It is quite possible in the Greek—the language Paul used to compose the 1 Timothy letter—to have a definite article before "childbearing". This phrase would then read, "the childbearing." "The childbearing" would likely be a reference to the birth of Christ who was promised to Eve as the seed who would crush the head of the serpent (Satan) in Genesis 3. Jesus—who is the fulfillment of this promise—came into the world through the womb of a faithful woman, Mary. It was this same faithful woman who would raise and instruct this boy who would eventually grow up to die for our sin and rise again so that all of humanity could be made new and so that, through Him, there would no longer be "Jew nor Gentile, slave nor free, male nor female, for all are one in Christ Jesus"

---

20 Editor, James R. Beck, *Two Views on Women in Ministry* (Grand Rapids, MI: Zondervan Academic, 2005), 90.

(Galatians 3:28). Women, like men, are saved by "The" birth, death and resurrection of Christ, if they "continue in faith, love and holiness with propriety" (1 Timothy 2:15b).

A Closing Word

Throughout this work we have tried to gently challenge the exegesis commonly used to support a view that restricts women in ministry. Nevertheless, we hope it is clear that we have so much love in our hearts for our brothers and sisters serving in churches where they hold a more restrictive view toward women in ministry. We are incredibly thankful for the Gospel work they are doing and we happily recognize that what unites us is infinitely greater than what divides us because Jesus is at the center of everything we are building. Many of our friends who hold a more restrictive view of women in church leadership (based primarily on their reading of 1 Timothy 2) still affirm women in many areas of ministry and would typically believe that:

Women can teach Bible classes in Christian colleges to men and women.

Women can write blog posts and scholarly articles.

Women can read scripture in public.

Women can share from scripture in conjunction with their missionary work when the church is gathered; they can lead, preach and teach in other parts of the world as missionaries, and prophecy when the church is gathered.

Women can teach children, and instruct youth boys and girls until a certain age (though we are not certain what that age should be, regarding boys/men, especially since we are told that adolescence has been extended into the late twenties!).

Women can write theological books that are intended to instruct men and women about gender roles, expounding the authoritative scriptures.

A woman can teach the Bible authoritatively during a Monday evening seminar, or during a conference, to a crowd of men and women.[21]

Women can do all of this and more!

Yet women cannot, according to a certain reading of 1 Timothy 2, teach from the word of God, exercising authority over men, when the church is gathered as a body of believers. When taken seriously, this approach leads to all kinds of strange inconsistencies.

Sarah Sumner highlights some in her book, *Men and Women in the Church*:

> A woman can step into a foreign mission field and evangelize an unreached people. She can disciple a king, rebuke a false teacher, correct a wayward brother, and change the course of history by her prayers. She can lead or preach to thousands as long as the appropriate men invite her to. If her leadership is more suited for work outside the church, then she can become a senator, CEO or even president. There's really nothing she can't do.
>
> On the other hand, every Christian woman is told not to lead too much. She can lead women, but mustn't be called the women's pastor. She can preach to men in someone's home or in a conference setting but not in a local sanctuary. She can oversee a big budget in a big government or nonprofit, but she

---

21 I'm thinking here of Kathy Keller's wonderful little book, *Jesus, Justice and Gender Roles* and the position she defends.

> can't have an official say over the small budget of a small church. Are women supposed to believe that these vast and pervasive inconsistencies are justified by orthodox Christian theology?[22]

Do you feel the strange inconsistencies and somewhat arbitrary line-drawing that is taking place above? Are men and women supposed to believe that these "vast and pervasive inconsistencies" are warranted from a fair and thorough reading of scripture?

Some theologians who want to reserve leadership, pastoral ministry and the teaching of God's Word to men only have addressed the above inconsistencies by deciding that women should *not* teach men at church, in Bible College/Seminary, or in a parachurch ministry.[23] Some have even gone a step further to suggest that women should probably not lead men in the business sphere or political arena, or in any situation where authority is being exercised over a man, because the Biblical teachings on headship and authority are rooted in creation, not just church governance, and to reverse the God-ordained roles for men and women in any area of life will put a strain on their humanity.[24] This has been applied by popular pastors and theologians (e.g. John Piper and Wayne Grudem to name two prominent

---

22 Sarah Sumner, *Men and Women in the Church* (Downers Grove, Ill: Intervarsity Press, 2003), 26.

23 John Piper appears to take this view. See https://relevantmagazine.com/culture/john-piper-interview-women-not-pastoring-twitter-user-inspires-christians-name-christian-women-teachers-leaders/

24 I (Chris) heard J.I. Packer claimed something very similar to this in a Q and A at Regent College. And the above claim is a reasonable inference to draw from a complementarian view of the 'creation principle'. Wayne Grudem makes a similar move in his book *Evangelical Feminism.*

examples[25]) to mean that a woman should likely not be a police officer, or a referee in a sports contest involving men; she shouldn't have a male secretary, and she should give directions in a way that honours the leadership of men. Basically she should not be in any position in which she exercises authority over a man because that will put a strain on their God-given nature and humanity. After all, according to the restrictive argument based on 1 Timothy 2 this is not just a church thing, it is a creation thing. Those who want to restrict it to *just* a church thing are not really being consistent with the argument they are making about the created order. This view, as off-putting as it may sound to many Christians, is at least consistent. But now we are faced with the problem of a position that is even more restrictive toward the roles of women than the Bible itself. Think, for example, about the leadership of Deborah in the book of Judges! This view also creates uncomfortable questions: for example, based on these restrictions, at what point am I (Elita) unable to teach my three sons? Will they reach a certain age (my oldest is almost 15 at this writing) when I will no longer be permitted to teach them scriptural doctrine in my home because it would "put a strain on their God-given authority"?

These are good questions.

As far as we can tell, the options are that you either (1) become more restrictive than the Bible itself for the sake of consistency; (2) live in the strange, inconsistent space detailed above where lines are drawn in seemingly arbitrary places; or (3) move in an egalitarian direction. We are arguing for this third option and

---

25 Ed. John Piper & Wayne Grudem, *Recovering Biblical Manhood and Womanhood: Response to Evangelical Feminism* (Wheaton, ILL: Crossway Publishers, 1991) See Chapter on A Vision of Biblical Complementarity 31-59.

we sincerely hope you reject the first option and find the second increasingly more unlivable. There is room at the table for men and women to lead, teach and pastor the church and, when it *does* happen, the *whole* church can flourish.

SPOTLIGHT:

A BRIEF HISTORY OF WOMEN IN MINISTRY

······ Elita ······

In a letter dated February 5, 1675, Sir Isaac Newton penned these now-famous words: “If I have seen further, it is by standing on the shoulders of giants.”[1]

If it’s true that every generation stands on the shoulders of its previous generation—and I believe it is—then tracing our heritage is important. As a woman involved in ministry, I have felt a particular responsibility to not only honour what scripture has to say regarding the role of women in the church, but also to pay close attention to what history has to teach us on this subject. The general consensus within the modern church seems to accept the notion of women in ministry as being a relatively “new idea”; that the inclusion of women in church leadership roles should be considered a nod to our current cultural climate and a likely result of feminism infiltrating the church. At least, this was the narrative I had come to believe.

Growing up in the southern United States, no one sat me down as a young girl and explained appropriate gender roles within the church. No one told me what men could do, what women couldn’t do, or vice versa. I simply came to understand, through my own observation, that the natural order placed men in leadership roles—as pastors, elders, deacons, etc. If women did have a “primary” leadership role, it was almost always leading

---

1 This quote was made famous by Sir Isaac Newton in a letter written to his colleague, Robert Hook. The original letter remains in trust by the Historical Society of Pennsylvania.

other women or teaching Sunday school. Mind you, I didn't—and still don't—necessarily think this was wrong. After all, many women legitimately feel called and gifted to serve other women or teach children in Sunday school. However, I suppose the real reason I never thought twice about the difference in roles at my particular church was because, at least to my knowledge, no one was being sidelined as a result of their gender. But with the dramatic rise of women in pastoral and/or church leadership over the last twenty plus years, many men and women—myself included—have been left grappling with what has felt like a revolutionary adjustment in church culture.

While it can be tempting to think we are living in a generation that is only just seeing women rise into ministerial leadership positions, the facts tell us otherwise. The exciting reality is that for generations, though not often highlighted in history, women have repeatedly risen into church leadership roles. In fact, a brief look into church history reveals that while men have traditionally dominated church life, women leaders have continuously re-emerged during renewal movements in the church.

In the well-researched book, *Women In The Church,* Denise Muir Kjesbo digs into this re-emergence of female leaders within the church. According to Kjesbo, certain historians decided to investigate this compelling rise and fall of women in church leadership and their findings are fascinating. Their research reveals this interesting historical pattern to which our generation should pay particular attention: renewal movements initially open the door to greater female involvement, allowing men and women to serve side-by-side, only to shut the door as churches become institutionalized and seek respectability in the broader culture.[2] To put it in layman's terms, their research shows that when revival happens women are involved, but when the church wants to become an official organization women are sidelined.

Dr. Roberta Hestenes—the first tenured female professor in the School of Theology at Fuller Seminary—used this same research in her dissertation, suggesting that "women played crucial roles in the initial pioneering stages of religious movements only to be replaced by men as the movements became more 'respectable.'" According to Hestenes, this phenomenon occurs through a three-stage process:

1. The Charismatic Phase

During the charismatic phase, the early days of revival movements, women serve as evangelists, church planters, and teachers. This first generation inevitably passes the baton to the second and third generation of leaders who begin to desire the respectability of credential holders. As this occurs, the charismatic phase gives way to the next phase.

2. The Credentialing Phase

This takes various forms, but is often defined by a push for higher education and ordination. Neither of these are wrong; however, until more recent years, both have discriminated against women, making it almost impossible for females to gain credentials. This then leads to the third phase.

3. The Institutionalizing Phase

This final phase is the desire for full institutional respectability.

---

2 Stanley J. Grenz and Denise Muir Kjesbo, *Women In the Church* (InterVarsity Press, Downers Grove, IL, 1995), 37.

As members of the movement desire acceptance by other, respectable denominations, most of which do not approve of female leadership, women are increasingly excluded from positions of responsibility.[3]

This three-stage process can be seen in several renewal movements throughout recent history but for the sake of space, we will consider only one: the Sunday School Movement.

The Sunday School Movement was a creative outlet for women in the nineteenth century in the United States. It grew out of a concern for underprivileged children who worked such long hours during the week (back in the days of child labour) that they could not participate in public education. Because the ministers were often opposed to teaching literacy skills in the churches, it was left mostly to the women. Despite opposition from the men, the movement grew (The Charismatic Phase). Soon the male leadership co-opted the movement, forming the 'American Sunday School Union' (The Credentialing Phase). The men set the policy and governed the organization while the women, who composed the majority of the teachers, did the grassroots work. As the movement gained respectability and became established, women effectively handed over the reins of leadership to the men (The Institutionalizing Phase). Thus, institutionalization virtually eliminated women from leadership positions within an important area of the church's ministry.[4]

This repeated marginalization of women within the church is an interesting, and sad, historical trend to consider. Thankfully,

---

3 As cited by Stanley J. Grenz and Denise Muir Kjesbo, *Women In the Church*, 37-39.

4 Grenz, 45.

this pattern doesn't tell the whole story. I have been greatly encouraged to learn of women in previous generations who, though often unable to function in traditional church settings, still found ways to utilize their God-given gifts as missionaries, church revitalizers and ministry lay leaders. For example, Susanna Wesley, mother of John and Charles Wesley (co-founders of the Methodist Church) opened her home up to a Sunday evening Bible study in the early 1700s. What was originally meant for teaching her ten young children began to attract more and more neighbours until eventually there were 200 people attending regularly. It is likely due to his mother's influence on his life that John Wesley himself endorsed a woman, Mrs. Sarah Crosby, as a lay preacher in June 1771, saying she had an "extraordinary call". He also gave his stamp of approval to Mary Bosanquet. Both Crosby and Bosanquet became tireless evangelists, and some 41 women eventually became lay preachers in the 1700s.[5]

Another example worth noting is a woman by the name of Phoebe Palmer who, during the 19th century, began a women's prayer meeting each Tuesday afternoon with her sister. These "successful prayer meetings inspired similar gatherings around the country, bringing Christians of many denominations together to pray. Phoebe soon found herself in the limelight—the most influential woman in the largest, fastest-growing religious group in America."[6] She went on to serve as one of the first officers of the Ladies Home Missionary Society, was a founder of the Five Points Mission in New York, was responsible for the establishment of a mission in China and was instrumental in

---

5 Jennifer Woodruff Tait, "I Received My Commission From Him, Brother," www.christianitytoday.com, accessed January 10, 2020.

6 Christianity Today, Issue 82, "Phoebe Palmer: Mother of the Holiness Movement", www.christianitytoday.com, accessed January 21, 2020.

the establishment of both Garrett Biblical Institute and Drew Theological Seminary.[7] She preached unapologetically, though certainly aware of the waves she was making because of her gender, and her revival work took her through Canada, the United States and Britain where she saw approximately 25,000 people converted to Christianity.

One final illustration is the life of Francis Willard (1839 -1898), the founder and long-term president of the World's Woman's Christian Temperance Union. Dwight L. Moody, one of the most popular evangelists of his day, asked Francis to assist him in his evangelistic work. She thoroughly loved this work and Moody encouraged her to preach temperance and suffrage as well as the Gospel. Through her connection with him, she reached thousands of people she otherwise would have never touched.[8]

What, then, can we learn from this history? I humbly suggest we allow it to do two things: encourage us and teach us. If the involvement of women in church ministry historically means renewal is on the rise, we—the global, 21st century church—should be expectant and excited when gifted female leaders emerge. May we also learn from this history—avoiding marginalizing one gender for the sake of acceptance and instead seeking to honour, develop and steward the gifts God has purposely given His people, both men and women, for His name's sake in our generation. "So in Christ Jesus you are all children of God through faith...there is neither Jew nor Gentile, neither slave nor free, nor is there male and female, for you are all one in Christ Jesus" (Galatians 3:26, 28).

---

7 Ernest Wall, "I Commend Unto You Phoebe", *Religion In Life*, Vol. 26 (Summer, 1957), 398.

8 Ray Strachey, *Francis Willard: Her Life and Work* (New York: Fleming H. Revell, 1913), 208.

CONCLUSION

········· Elita & Chris

I (Elita) was recently chatting with a female friend who had, for some time, felt called into church ministry. She shared with me the struggle, the uphill battle and the heartache that had spanned the better part of 20 years. Unfortunately, hers is an all-too-common story among women who have longed to serve in the church:

> I did everything I knew to do. I followed the same path as my Christian brothers. I served in the church. I volunteered countless hours away from my husband and family. I got my Master's degree concentrating on Theology. I sought help. I asked for experience. But over and over again it was as though the men in leadership at my church just didn't know what to make of me. When I asked for mentoring or discipleship, I

> was repeatedly told they couldn't help me. They considered my not feeling called to serve in children's ministry or women's ministry as entirely 'out-of-the-box'. Were they threatened? Did they assume I was there with some sort of underlying feminist agenda? I wish so badly they could have known I just wanted to help and contribute whatever gifts God has given me for the sake of the Gospel.

She was quick to point out the beautifully redemptive side of her story as well: "If it wasn't for the few men who championed me, I would have given up a long time ago. But those men gave me courage and called out the gifts in me. I just wonder if men know they have such a powerful voice in how women actually get empowered?" She eventually chose to use her degree and her giftings outside the church.

As I sat there listening to her, the reality hit me that the continued stonewalling of women *within* the church will force them to use their gifts *outside* the church.

Unfortunately, my friend's story is not an exception to the rule; rather, it is a commonly felt reality for far too many gifted women within the church. It is stories like hers that compel us not to skirt around this touchy subject, but to dive-in and face the discomfort of it. Our hope is that this generation of men and women will do the deep groundwork that ultimately paves a way for the next generation of men and women in the church.

We are mindful that as deeply personal as it is for some, this conversation represents a point of continuing disagreement within the body of Christ. Hopefully, it is a disagreement we can discuss and debate while not dividing the body or getting distracted from the disciple-making mission that Jesus has given to us. And if we disagree, we do so with gentleness and love. We believe that the argument of this short book is the best way to read the specific texts we've looked at and that it captures well the general thrust of the New Testament regarding women in leadership. It is important to reiterate that we love and work with other brothers and sisters and churches who hold to a different perspective, and they are more than welcome to attend our church.

In the end, it is appropriate to finish this book by quoting again these powerful words which we included earlier, as they capture the heart behind these pages:

To those in the next generation of women who have sensed a call on their life, but have felt conflicted or confused over the role of women in the church, I pray this book breathes fresh life into you. May you feel encouraged to lean into the gifts God has put inside of you, seeking to steward them well. Being a woman in no way excuses us from treating the call to teach or pastor as anything less than holy; all who feel a call to teach should be committed to learning and growing and sitting under sound theological teaching. And though the idea of women in leadership may remain a tough subject within the church, and though it may feel like an uphill battle at times, may you and I both remember that God did not make a mistake when He put the gift of leadership inside of us. But let us also remember that we have an opportunity before us to be a generation of women who don't rise because men fall. Rather, let us set a new standard that seeks to honor men. It is not us against them. It is us with them for the sake of the Gospel. Who knows? Perhaps—like Esther—we were created for such a moment as this.

FAQ

QUESTION:

Isn't the position argued for in this booklet the result of being influenced by western culture's view of women and gender equality?

RESPONSE:

This is a great question and a very real concern in our hearts. It is clear that cultural pressures can cause people to distort the word of God; but they can also cause us to go back to Scripture and see if we missed something, or were misreading certain passages. It should be clear that the argument in this book is an argument based on scripture because, in the end, the question that matters most to us is, what is the most faithful reading of the text according to genre, context, and authorial intent, as far as it is discernible to us?

It is also important to keep in mind that cultural pressure comes from all different directions. Secularism and feminism, for certain. But also family, tradition, tribal affiliations and the doctrine of the church you grew up in. We all swim in a confluence of cultural forces. In this instance, it is not some monolithic entity labelled "culture" that has caused us to reevaluate scripture and empower women in all areas of church leadership, nor is it an extreme feminism that would seek to collapse all gender distinctions, which is a position we do not hold. Though gender expression is often culturally relative to time and space (for example, one hundred years ago pink was considered the colour for boys, not blue!) and may become overly narrow and constraining in an unhelpful manner, we believe men and women are different physiologically and biologically and those differences are good and beneficial. Instead, it is scripture, and we would argue[1], the influence of scripture in culture, that is causing us to reevaluate a certain reading of scripture that may unduly restrict women in the exercising of their God-given spiritual gifts.

The above is also a partial answer to those who are concerned that this booklet represents some kind of liberal, theological agenda that ends up being a slippery slope in the life of the

---

1 It can be persuasively argued that apart from the existence of God as a foundation for objective moral values, the concept of the *image of God* possessed equally by both male and female, and the writings of Paul elsewhere that contend that male and female are equal in Christ, the affirmation of the equality of the sexes across cultures and time periods as a moral absolute has no logically consistent leg to stand on. The Greek philosophers are of no real help, atheistic Darwinism is worse, and humanism is just the Christian teaching of human dignity stripped of its logical foundation. In other words, it is the influence of the Christian Gospel and the teachings of the New Testament that has caused us to react negatively towards the concept of inequality.

church. It is not a liberal agenda; it is a Biblical, New Covenant agenda, in-synch with the Spirit and the liberating nature of God's kingdom.

QUESTION:

What are the two distinct positions in this debate?

RESPONSE:

There are two primary positions held in evangelical churches: complementarianism and egalitarianism. Neither position can fairly be called the "traditional position." Often the complementarian perspective will claim the support of church tradition. However, when one reads the actual positions, statements and exegesis of many of the prominent church fathers on these debated texts (Tertuallian and Augustine, for example) one will quickly recognize that modern complementarians have rejected or revised their approaches, rhetoric, and conclusions significantly and are, in that sense, also revising the "traditional position".

More than that, complementarians have introduced several novel interpretations over the last 60 years or so. Kevin Giles in his book, *What the Bible Actually Teaches on Women*, highlights these exegetical innovations: "Their focus on 'roles' is a recent invention. The way they explain away Junias' ministry as an apostle is novel. The subordinationist use of the Trinity to talk about Father/Son and male/female relationships is unprecedented and a strange theological innovation."[2] He goes on to

---

2 Kevin Giles, *What the Bible Actually Teaches On Women*, 174

say that, in actuality, "Complementarian forms of exegesis have taken shape since the 1960s to support moden complementarian theologies and church structures."[3] The above (debatable) points are given, not to be unnecessarily combative but, rather, to level the playing field between the two positions by creating greater caution when we claim the 'historic' or 'traditional' position for our side of the debate.

That being said, the complementarian position holds that men and women are created equal yet with different roles and callings from God. When it comes to ministry within the body of Christ all women are spiritually gifted by God and all positions of leadership are open to women with the single exception of overseer (synonymous with the term elder or bishop in scripture). Often people in this camp believe that a woman cannot be a pastor exercising spiritual authority over men. Or, at the very least, women should not lead or teach men in the church.

The Egalitarian position holds that, though men and women may be distinctly different in various ways, gender has no bearing regarding what position a person can hold within the church. Our position still upholds the uniqueness of the sexes and refuses to collapse all gender distinctions or explain them away. But we believe that all positions of ministry are open to both qualified males and females equally, including the position of pastor and elder. More than that, the church benefits greatly when women operate in their giftings as pastors and teachers. Though one may quibble with the details of the above definitions, and there is certainly a sliding scale of sorts when it comes to both positions (i.e: some churches being more "conservative" egalitarians while other congregations might lean more towards a softer

---

3 Kevin Giles, ibid., 174

complementarian perspective), in broad strokes at least, this is what we mean by the terms.

QUESTION:

If we approached all of the Bible the way this booklet approaches the passage in 1 Timothy 2 most Bible readers would be completely lost. How could a lay person ever trust that they were correctly understanding the New Testament?

RESPONSE:

We understand this concern and take it very seriously. Keep in mind that scripture is sufficiently clear in matters pertaining to our salvation. But that doesn't mean that all parts of scripture are equally clear. You need not be a scholar to understand the simple truths of the Gospel, but there are some difficult parts to Paul's writings, which lead to disagreement in the church. Even Peter thought Paul could be difficult because he wrote in 2nd Peter,

> Bear in mind that our Lord's patience means salvation, just as our dear brother Paul also wrote you with the wisdom that God gave him. He writes the same way in all his letters, speaking in them of these matters. His letter contains some things that are hard to understand, which ignorant and unstable people distort, as they do the other scriptures, to their own destruction.
>
> 2 Peter 3:15,16

Not only does Peter put Paul's writing on the same level as other scripture here, he acknowledges that Paul is not always easy to understand. If Peter had difficulty, is it surprising that we might occasionally struggle two thousand years later? We think not. There are, of course, some occasions where being a scholar, or reading scholars, with a working knowledge of Biblical Greek, is very helpful. 1st Timothy 2 is one such occasion and this is why well-meaning, humble and learned theologians, who love Jesus and submit to the authority of His word offer different interpretations of this passage.

QUESTION:

What is your view of 1 Corinthians 11:2-16 and Paul's reference to the creation story in this passage?

RESPONSE:

Here is the passage in question:

> I praise you for remembering me in everything and for holding to the traditions just as I passed them onto you. But I want you to realize that the head of every man is Christ, and the head of woman is man, and the head of Christ is God. Every man who prays or prophesies with his head covered dishonours his head. But every woman who prays or prophesies with her head uncovered dishonours her head—it is the same as having her head shaved. For if a woman does not cover her head, she might as well have her hair cut off: but if it is a disgrace for a woman to have her hair cut off or her head shaved, then she should

> cover her head. A man ought not to cover his head, since he is the image and glory of God: but woman is the glory of man. For man did not come from woman, but woman from man; neither was man created for woman, but woman for man. It is for this reason that a woman ought to have authority over her own head, because of the angels. Nevertheless, in the Lord woman is not independent of man, nor is man independent of woman. For as woman came from man, so also man is born of woman. But everything comes from God. Judge for yourselves: Is it proper for a woman to pray to God with her head uncovered? Does not the very nature of things teach you that if a man has long hair, it is a disgrace to him, but that if a woman has long hair, it is her glory? For long hair is given to her as a covering. If anyone wants to be contentious about this, we have no other practice—nor do the churches of God.

This passage does not mention women preachers or pastors or leaders. It doesn't say women can't be pastors or preachers. So whatever you think this passage means, it shouldn't be used to sideline women in ministry. In fact, it supports women praying and prophesying in the congregation.

What it does say, however, remains very dense and difficult to understand. The mysteries that remain, include sentences like: "It is for this reason that a woman ought to have authority over her own head, because of the angels." What is the connection between a head covering and the "angels"? Who are the angels and why should the woman be concerned with them? Or, " Does not the very nature of things teach you that if a man has long hair, it is a disgrace to him, but that if a woman has long hair, it is her glory?" How does the nature of things relate to or teach us that long hair is disgraceful to a man and short hair is disgraceful to a woman? These types of statements have caused many commentators to scratch their heads in befuddlement.

Our experience with these particular verses has gone something like this: We might become convinced of one interpretation, only to study another and find that the conclusions we'd so confidently landed on were riddled through with exegetical problems. If you haven't had a similar experience with these verses we would encourage you to keep reading! Here are some of the more difficult parts of the passage that have kept Bible commentators busy.

First, how do we understand the word 'head'? The Greek word translated as head is *kephale* and it can mean "ruler" or "or one in authority" but it can also mean "first principle" or "source" or "origin." It is not at all necessary to read *kephale* as meaning "ruler" or "one in authority" in this passage, as many scholars have pointed out. Instead it can be read as "source" without doing violence to the text. More than that, understanding the Greek word *kephale* as meaning "source" makes better sense of the passage. To quote Graham Joseph Hill,

God is the 'source' of Christ in that he was begotten in the virgin Mary. Christ is the 'source' of man in that Christ was involved in creation. Man is the 'source' of woman in that Genesis tells us that Eve was called 'woman', because she was taken out of man. If we consider *kephale* as meaning 'source' or 'origin' then there is nothing in this text which hinders women from ministering in pastoral or teaching or prophetic roles.[4]

Another tricky interpretive puzzle is how does one justify

---

4 Graham Joseph Hill, *Holding Up Half the Sky* (Eugene, OR: Wipf & Stock publishers, 2020), 47.

Paul's reading of the creation story? He writes, "A man ought not to cover his head, since he is the image and glory of God; but the woman is the glory of man." (1 Corinthians 11:7). Paul makes it sound as though only the man is made in the image of God, whereas the woman is made in the image of man, actually contradicting the teaching of Genesis 1:27! This type of hierarchy is not naturally taught or implied by Genesis 1 or 2, and this type of exegetical move is very hard to justify from the actual Genesis text.

Moreover, Paul makes a statement at the end of this passage of scripture where he writes, "Nevertheless, in the Lord woman is not independent of man, nor is man independent of woman. For as woman came from man, so also man is born of woman. But everything comes from God" (1 Corinthians 11:11). Here Paul uses the very significant phrase "in the Lord", testifying to a new reality that Christ has brought about. In doing so he heads in the direction of equality and a level playing field because the new reality that arises from being "in the Lord" seems to overthrow Paul's previous comments that are often quoted to support some kind of hierarchy. This has led some commentators to conclude that in this passage Paul is quoting an erroneous view held by the Corinthian church and when he writes "in the Lord" he was correcting the wrong view. This approach is made plausible by the fact that, elsewhere in the letter, Paul is doing this very thing. Examples include 1 Corinthians 6:12,13 and few other sections in the letter. Though this represents a minority view, Lucy Peppiat argues convincingly for it in her book, *Unveiling Paul's Women*, presenting many arguments (not all of which we find convincing) with the accumulative force of making the above reading compelling—though, again, it is a conclusion that should be held tentatively.

More commonly, others point out that Paul is actually concerned about gender distinctions being upheld in the worship and attire of men and women at Corinth. Paul had very likely taught the church that, in Christ, "there is no longer male or female." Perhaps this is the tradition Paul is referring to at the beginning of this passage. It is possible that men and women were applying this tradition in such a way that the women, in particular, were casting off all restraint by letting their hair down (uncovering their head) and acting in such a way that would have brought disrepute on the Gospel and sent the wrong message to the surrounding culture while also, potentially, dishonouring their husbands. In fact, some scholars point out that, in those days, it was often prostitutes who went around with their hair uncovered in public. To quote N.T. Wright, "This isn't suggested directly here, but it may have been in the back of his mind. If the watching world discovered that the Christians were having meetings where women 'let their hair down' in this fashion, it could have the same effect on their reputation as it would in the modern West if someone looked into a church and found the women all wearing bikinis."[5]

Though much of what Paul writes is opaque to us and, though his reasoning appears obscure given the cultural distance separating us from the situation in Corinth, it is possible that this is the general meaning or thrust of the passage.

Regardless of what conclusions you draw on the basis of this scripture, we don't believe it should be used to sideline or silence women in leadership in the modern church.

---

5 N.T. Wright, *Paul for Everyone: 1 Corinthians* (Louisville, KY:John Knox Press, 2004), 140, 141.

QUESTION:

Doesn't the fact that Paul assumes that all the elders are male in 1 Timothy 3:1-8 and Titus 1:6-10 lead to the conclusion that the practice of selecting only male elders should be the standard for the church today?

RESPONSE:

This is a great question that gives a lot of people pause when reading English translations of the Bible. Friends of ours have suggested that only men should be pastors or elders based on the fact that in English translations of 1 Timothy 3, it seems as though Paul uses the male pronoun when discussing elders. We need to be careful what kind of conclusions we base on this. Paul could mean that only men should be elders. Or he could be writing to a group of male elders at the church in Ephesus, without intending to imply that a woman can never be an elder. Either way, the use of the male pronoun in our English translations doesn't tell us a whole lot here and is certainly too flimsy to build on it a case for an all male eldership, for all times. When Paul writes that an elder should be a husband of one wife he is very likely writing against polygamy and adultery. This is a statement no more intended to exclude women as it is intended to exclude single men. In fact, if we read it as excluding single men, Jesus and the apostle Paul wouldn't be allowed to serve as elders in the church! As Hill writes, "This 'one woman man' phrase does not exclude married women from these roles, nor does it exclude single women and men. If managing a household is a requirement for entry into these roles, then Paul and Jesus don't qualify. Nor do many of the great leaders of the church throughout its history."[6]

It is also important to note that, other than Paul mentioning that an elder should only be a husband to one wife, the male pronoun does not appear in this passage at all. The translators have inserted it. The Greek male pronoun is *autos.* And I repeat—it doesn't appear anywhere in this passage. The Greek word that does appear at the beginning of 1 Timothy 3 is *Tis,* which means anyone and is not gender specific. *Anyone* who aspires to be an elder aspires to a noble thing.

In the end, the 1 Timothy 3 passage (and the corresponding one found in Titus 1) describes the type of person an elder should be (temperate, self-controlled, gentle not quarrelsome, not a lover of money, etc.); this passage is not about gender, but about character and competency. Character is what matters regarding leadership roles in the church such as eldership. And character is what still matters today, making Paul's instruction just as applicable and binding in the modern context as it was when he wrote it to the early church in Ephesus. Therefore, qualified women should not be forbidden from taking on this role in the church.

---

6 Graham Joseph Hill, *Holding Up Half the Sky: A Biblical Case for Women Leading and Teaching in the Church* (Eugene, OR: Wipf & Stock Publishing, 2020), 58.

BIBLIOGRAPHY

Craig Bloomberg, *The NIV Application Commentary: 1 Corinthians* (Grand Rapids, MI: Zondervan Publishing, 1994)

Craig Skeener, *Paul, Women, and Wives: Marriage and Women's Ministry in the Letters of Paul* (Peabody, Mass: Hendrickson, 1992)

Don Williams, *The Apostle Paul and Women in the Church* (Glendale, CA: Regal, 1977)

Editor, James R. Beck, *Two Views of Women in Ministry* (Grand Rapids, MI: Zondervan Academic, 2005)

Graham Joseph Hill, *Holding Up Half the Sky: A Biblical Case for Women Leading and Teaching in the Church* (Eugene, OR: Wipf & Stock Publishing, 2020_

Gregory A. Boyd and Paul R. Eddy, *Across the Spectrum: Understanding Issues in Evangelical Theology* (Grand Rapids, MI: Baker Academic, 2009)

Gordon D. Fee, *1 and 2 Timothy, Titus, New International Biblical Commentary* (Peabody, Mass: Hendrickson, 1992)

General Editors Ronald W. Pierce & Rebecca Merrill Groothuis, *Discovering Biblical Equality: Complementarity without Hierarchy* (Downers Grove, Ill: Intervarsity Press, 2004)

Iain Provan, *Seriously Dangerous Religion* (Waco, TX: Baylor University Press, 2014)

John Temple Bristow, *What Paul Really Said About Women* (New York, NY: HarperCollins Publishing, 1991)

Dickson, John, *Hearing Her Voice* (Grand Rapids, MI: Zondervan Publishing, 2012)

J. Lee Grady, *Ten Lies the Church Tells Women* (Lake Mary, FL: Creation House, 2000)

John G. Stackhouse Jr., *Partners In Christ: A Conservative Case for Egalitarianism* (Downers Grove, Ill: InterVarsity Press, 2015)

John Stott, *The Message of 1 and 2 Timothy & Titus* (Downers Grove, Ill: Inter-Varsity Press, 1996)

John Stott, *The Message of 1 Timothy & Titus* (Downers Grove, Ill: Inter-Varsity Press, 1996)

Kari Torjesen Malcolm, *Women at the Crossroads* (Downers Grove, Ill: InterVarsity, 1982)

Kate Cooper, *Band of Angels: The Forgotten World of Early Christian Women* (New York, NY: Overlook Press, 2013)

Kathy Keller, *Jesus, Justice and Gender Roles* (Grand Rapids, MI: Zondervan Publishing, 2014)

Kevin Giles, *What the Bible Actually Teaches On Women* (Eugene, OR: Cascades Books, 2018)

R.T. France, *Women in the Church's Ministry: A Test Case for Biblical Interpretation* (Grand Rapids, MI: William B. Eerdmans Publishing Company, 1995)

Richard & Catherine Kroeger, *I Suffer Not a Woman: Rethinking 1 Timothy 2:11-15 in Light of Ancient Evidence* (Grand Rapids, MI: Baker, 1992)

Loren Cunningham & David Joel Hamilton, *Why Not Women?* (Seattle, WA: YWAM Publishing, 2000)

Mark Driscoll, *Who Do You Think You Are? Finding Your True Identity in Christ* (Nashville, TN: Thomas Nelson Publishing, 2013)

Mark Driscoll, *On Church Leadership* (Wheaton, Ill: Crossway, 2008)

N.T. Wright, *Paul For Everyone: The Pastoral Letters: 1 and 2 Timothy* (Downers Grove, Ill: Intervarsity Press, 2009)

N.T. Wright, *Paul for Everyone: 1 Corinthians* (Louisville, KY:-John Knox Press, 2004)

Lucy Peppiat, *Unveiling Paul's Women: Making Sense of 1 Corinthians 11:2-16* (Eugene, OR: Wifi & Stock, 2018).

Lucy Peppiat, *Rediscovering Scriptures Vision for Women* (Downers Grove, ILL: IVP Academic, 2019)

Paul Barnett, *1 Corinthians: Holiness and Hope of a Rescued People* (Scotland, TW: Christian Focus, 2000)

John Piper & Wayne Grudem, *Recovering Biblical Manhood & Womanhood: A Response to Evangelical Feminism* (Wheaton, Ill: Crossway Publishing, 1991)

Scot McKnight, *The Blue Parakeet: Rethinking How You Read the Bible* (Grand Rapids, MI: Zondervan, 2008)

Stanley J. Grenz and Denise Muir Kjesbo, *Women In the Church* (InterVarsity Press, Downers Grove, IL, 1995)

Walter L. Liefeld, *1 & 2 Timothy/Titus: The NIV Application Commentary* (Grand Rapids, MI: Zondervan, 1999)

Wayne Grudem, *Evangelical Feminism: A New Path to Liberalism* (Wheaton, Ill: Crossway Publishing, 2006)

Manufactured by Amazon.ca
Bolton, ON

20161237R00074